# Managing WITH People

## A Manager's Handbook of
## Organization Development Methods

# Managing WITH People

## A Manager's Handbook of
## Organization Development Methods

JACK K. FORDYCE
*Organization Development Consultant*

RAYMOND WEIL
*TRW Systems Group*

ADDISON-WESLEY PUBLISHING COMPANY
*Reading, Massachusetts*
*Menlo Park, California · London · Amsterdam · Don Mills, Ontario · Sydney*

Under the editorship of Warren G. Bennis

Cover design by Robert Shepard

ISBN 0-201-02103-X
KLMNOPQRST-AL-798

# Foreword

The appearance of *Managing WITH People* seems to me a significant landmark in the history of the maturing discipline—or way of life—that we call organization development (O.D.). Less than a decade ago, the practice of O.D. was almost entirely intuitive and experimental. We had to hack out the tools we needed. Now, only a few years later, the authors of *Managing WITH People* can classify many of the current principal tools of O.D. and describe the use of each article as if it were a hammer, a saw, or a drill.

As a participant in the pioneering days of O.D., I am pleased that much of what we so recently struggled to learn is already codified within these covers. I do not mean that anyone can lead or coach a major O.D. undertaking by a robotlike following of a set of instructions. The successful practice of O.D. will always demand skill, art, energy, luck, and personal authenticity and commitment of a high order.

Thinking of this book (especially Part Three) as a box of tools is helpful to me. A saw and a hammer in the hands of a journeyman carpenter are considerably more effective than in mine. Nevertheless, I can cut wood with a saw and I can drive nails with a hammer. They are not mysterious to me. Day by day, I can learn to use them more skillfully—and I can build many things that I want to build.

The toolbox of O.D. is by no means complete. We shall be steadily inventing and adding and replacing tools as time goes by.

I am pleased that Jack Fordyce and Raymond Weil were able to incorporate in this book much of what has been learned and tested so far at TRW Systems Group in Redondo Beach, California.

In 1962, a number of us in the Industrial Relations organization of TRW Systems Group were taking a hard look at training programs and career development activities. We had the advantage of consultation with several people associated with the NTL Institute, particularly Herbert A. Shepard, formerly with Case Western Reserve University, now associated with Yale University. Another major advantage was the inventiveness and openness to new ideas of many TRW executives. Key leadership and sanctioning roles have been played by R. F. Mettler, President of TRW Inc.; R. D. DeLauer, Executive Vice President and General Manager of TRW Systems Group; and J. E. Dunlap, Vice President–Human Relations of TRW Inc. Their determined support and direct involvement permitted us to experiment with several new programs aimed at helping individuals at TRW to function more effectively and in a more personally satisfying way than they had before.

In an early thought paper, Jim Dunlap and I expressed our sense of direction as follows:

"We can divide the kind of training that is required into two parts:

1. Training in specific skills. A particular employee . . . should have certain skills or knowledge . . . which are important for carrying out his job. In addition, since an individual cannot be an expert in depth in all these fields, it is quite important that he have a clear understanding of when he needs help . . . and where he can get this help. If he fails to realize his interdependence with respect to solving a particular problem, he will probably not call upon the

proper (company) resources to help him solve it. Therefore, his solution is not likely to be the best one the company is capable of producing.

2. Training in interpersonal and group membership skills . . . is important because of the crucial interdependencies within the organization. An individual is constantly interacting with many people above, below, and alongside of him in order to carry out his responsibilities. This kind of training involves the person developing his capacity to give and to receive help, to communicate and listen effectively, and to deal with people and organizational problems. In order to do this, an essential part of the process is that he critically examine his own theory and assumptions about people, organizations, and management."

A number of basic ideas suggested by this statement were developed, tested, and revised, and through this process became the techniques and approaches we now call by such names as Teambuilding, Intergroup, and Organization Mirror. They are now sufficiently standardized and predictable to be considered part of an emerging technology for human systems, generally known as organization development. In the last few years at TRW Systems, they have increasingly become a way of organizational life.

The key test for us has been whether a particular method was useful in a given specific instance for diagnosing and solving management problems. The history of O.D. at TRW saw an early emphasis on team-building for project teams and permanent organization units. In the last few years, the emphasis has shifted increasingly to intergroup problems, reaching out to include relationships with customers. Since the methods have been developed in response to perceived priorities, we have more experience with some of them than with others. However, we have had ample enough experience with all the applications described in *Managing WITH People* to know that they now constitute a dependable methodology.

Our experience has taught us that these techniques and approaches should be used organically, rather than mechanically. They should grow and change with organizational needs. We recognize, of course, that we need a plan, and that we must have some explicit strategy, but we try to do the particular things that are appropriate when they are needed and make sense. We try to think in terms of *emerging* sets of techniques that become part of the organizational culture.

The achievements of these kinds of programs have to be measured and seen in relative, not absolute, terms. The appropriate question is not, "Is our organization now 'open' as opposed to having been 'closed'?" It is far more realistic to ask, "Is our organization now more open than before, do our people show more trust in one another, and does that result in improved performance on the job?" We have found that a seemingly small improvement in some aspects of behavior has a great deal of impact on an organization. If an organization can move from a point where people spend one-tenth of their time in internecine combat to a point where they spend only one-twentieth of their time fighting one another, that organization has probably become more effective than the numbers indicate.

We should not wait for serious problems to erupt before we begin to apply the methods of *Managing WITH People* to our organizational situations. The key to getting started at all is to get started now. After all, it is only plain hard sense to begin making *good* existing team efforts better, and not to limit organization development activity to lifting obviously poor team performance to an acceptable level. Fighting fires can be a heroic business, but it is not the main business to which *Managing WITH People* addresses itself. The first admonition, then, is clear enough: BEGIN NOW WITH COMPE-TENT MANAGERS.

Second, we must keep in mind that the first steps we take are in fact first steps and by no means a complete and permanent solution. What makes the vital difference in O.D. activities is not a particular proven technique or even a collection of successful techniques—but rather *a long-term systematic effort to improve an organization's culture.* There is a tendency in organizations, certainly in American industrial organizations, to tinker with a single strand of their total cultures, and seek out magical, simple cures to complex human issues, rather than to deal comprehensively and continuously with the culture as a whole. Brainstorming (when it is pursued as a fad) comes to mind. How long does a "turned-on" participant of an occasional brain-storming session remain stimulated and innovation-minded after he steps back into his "normal" job atmosphere and frustrations? Or Management by Objectives: "Okay, we've gone through the Management by Objectives exercise headquarters sent out.  Now let's get back to our *real* work."

We must maintain the larger perspective of continuous organizational cultural change over a long period of time.  *Within* that perspective, first steps—taken *now*—are essential.

Sheldon A. Davis
Vice President and Director of
Industrial Relations
TRW Systems Group
Redondo Beach, California

# Preface

This handbook concentrates on the joint management of change and presents particular methods that have proven useful in this process.

The book is addressed to the manager who is curious about organization development (O.D.) and wants to learn more about it and to the manager who is already involved in an O.D. program and finds himself in need of a practical handbook of methodology and examples. Implicit in this presentation is our conviction that managers can and should take a more active role in an O.D. undertaking. We know many managers who have developed considerable skill in O.D. methods. While the consultant role is still necessary, we look forward to the day when a growing number of managers can function as consultants to one another. A massive move to more adaptive, effective, and human organization cultures is not possible until these understandings and skills become widespread. On the other hand, a brief presentation such as this necessarily oversimplifies. For this reason, we strongly recommend that the reader take advantage of the readings in the selected bibliography.

The book is also intended to be useful to students and may be of some value to practitioners in the field.

We do not attempt to define the field of organization development, the boundaries of which are rapidly expanding to include large-scale strategies of whole nations for social and economic change on the broadest level.

Many aspects of O.D. are merely touched on, including comprehensive systems of organizational diagnosis, training in concepts and skills, consultant-client relations, and various types of interventions.

We are indebted to: O. S. Farry, Manager of Organization Development at TRW Systems Group, for his direct contributions to this handbook; Sheldon A. Davis, Vice President and Director of Industrial Relations at TRW Systems Group, for fostering many of the ideas and methods presented here, as well as for his support; many TRW Systems Group staff people and consultants who have been actively engaged in this work for as long as a decade; Richard Beckhard of Richard Beckhard Associates and Massachusetts Institute of Technology, and Robert Tannenbaum of the University of California at Los Angeles for their critical review and valuable suggestions.

*November 1970*                                                         J.K.F.
                                                                        R.W.

# Contents

# Part One.  Move Over!

# What's Going On?

*"He not busy being born is busy dying."*

Bob Dylan

Wherever we look, institutions that once ruled extensive domains of property and influence now find their power waning. No longer in firm command of their markets, they are unable to meet their goals (whether to produce hard goods, train scholars, or save souls) and they are losing control of their human and physical resources.

The common cause of this falling away is the inability of the organization to respond robustly to changes in its environment. We may consider corporations to be more flexible and adaptive than churches, yet the death rate of corporations is exceedingly high. Fewer than a third of the 100 largest American corporations of 50 years ago are still doing business today.

As everyone knows, the rate of change has vastly accelerated in our time. This circumstance places a heavy responsibility on the management of every kind of enterprise. Change is the greatest threat to the survival of an organism or organization, and organizational survival is a primary responsibility of management.

Two particular changes in the world at large have had a strong impact on organizations: *new technology* and *new human expectations*. Organizational structures that were perfectly serviceable for the technology of World War II no longer work in the 1970's.

3

*"Our status quo has been knocked head over heels by the revolutions in science and technology, in transportation, in communication and the processing of information, in industry, agriculture and education, in demography and biomedical affairs. The swift pace of these revolutions makes it desperately necessary that our institutions be adaptable. When they are not, the sweep of events isolates them and dramatizes their anachronistic character."*

*John W. Gardner, December 1968*

In many fields that depend on advancing technology, the manager often lacks the knowledge to monitor, let alone direct, the flow of work. His employees are too highly educated in specialized fields. Without knowledge, he is unable to make sound decisions. The levers of power pass inevitably to the specialists.

Because of changes in human expectations (arising from affluence, more widespread education, and more rapid communications), people place a higher value on themselves than they used to, and feel that what they want is important and not to be lightly denied. This change has forced a migration of power from those who rule to those who participate. Our newspapers signal this effect daily.

Large groups of people who formerly trod their docile round of tasks now stir restlessly or protest riotously. The letter carriers kick up their heels. The teachers who teach our children obedience to the rules (among other things) disobediently picket the schools. That was supposed to be against the law. On many high school and college campuses, students flout established authority. The managers of education can scarcely take daily attendance.

From minority groups springs an insistent cry for autonomy over their own affairs. Blacks, reds, and chicanos refuse to abide the status quo. They are wresting power from the political managers who managed *them.*

People who serve or are served by a thousand institutions— religious, governmental, industrial, educational, military—insist that these institutions are blind to their needs. So power tends to slip downward into the hands of those who feel the need for change.

# Pope Hears Cardinal Challenge Emphasis on Papal Primacy

### BY LOUIS B. FLEMING
#### Times Staff Writer

ROME—Leo Josef Cardinal Sue-nens of Belgium, speaking Tuesday in the presence of Pope Paul VI, challenged what he called the excessive emphasis in the Roman Catholic Church on the primacy of the Pope.

He appealed instead for more power for the bishops and the exercise of authority by the bishops and the Pope as a "co-responsibili-ty."

Cardinal Suenens was one of 19 speakers at the second - working session of the Synod of Bishops called to advise the Pope on ways to improve the relationship between the Pontiff and the national episco-pal conferences and between the conferences themselves.

The speeches included:

—A proposal for a special commis-sion to study the function of public opinion within the church and its relationship to "sensus fidelium," the consensus of faith.

—A direct challenge to the Pope on the way he handled the "Huma-nae Vitae" birth control encyclical, coupled with an appeal for consulta-tions with the bishops before issuing any more encyclicals.

Thirty of the 146 bishops now have spoken, reflecting a clear division between those who place the empha-sis on the supreme authority of the Pope and those who place the emphasis on collegiality. The only

**Please Turn to Page 21, Col. 1**

## THE WEATHER

Light smog today.
U.S. Weather Bureau forecast: Mostly sunny today. Increasing high clouds tonight and partly cloudy and cool Thursday. High today, 74. High Tuesday, 71; low, 56.

Complete weather information on Part 2, Page 4.

## 1.   WHAT PEOPLE WANT

People don't seem to want what they used to want. The old deal isn't good enough.  And it is not only youth that feels this way, although its voice is clearest and strongest.

People don't want to do the same things over and over.  They want a chance to test and experience their individuality.  The surgeon at

40 has had enough of the operating room; he now wants to become a movie actor or a stockbroker.

People want greater freedom to do as they wish with their own bodies. They want to dress as they please or not dress, to wear their hair longer and grow beards, to experiment with drugs and sexuality. Women want to make their own decisions about abortion.

People want more *time* to express themselves—in art and in play.

As against western rationalism, many turn to oriental religion and mysticism, to exploration of their inner state through meditation and mood-altering chemicals. They want to *feel,* and to indulge the intuitive and spontaneous side of their nature.

People want their work to be challenging and interesting—they have for a long time, but more so now. Young people are often suspicious of established institutions of power and wealth. They believe that most organizations will destroy their individuality, which they feel to be both precious and perishable.

Many people are tired of hearing about political democracy while living in an oligarchy for 40 hours a week and being governed by corporate or institutional rules which were not of their making and which they lack power to change.

Young people want to make a significant contribution to peace, to conservation of natural resources, to population control, and to social justice. They are less drawn than the previous generation to the comforts of personal security and private consumption. One observer has commented on

> "... the rise of a new political class that behaves in a way the ancient Greeks considered aristocratic. Its members are not aristocratic by virtue of inherited wealth, high birth, or social status. Many, in fact, are of humble origin and proud of it. Their political behavior is aristocratic because they seek a meaningful public role that is not directly related to their own pecuniary interest. They have a strong notion of service, of political participation and of public—as opposed to private—good. They prefer to work in organizations in which they can feel themselves colleagues rather than subordinates. They have a strong distaste

*for hierarchal structures and when subjected to them—in the church, the university, the Army, or in government or corporate bureaucracy—they begin to press for reforms. They have a well-developed sense of privacy, of tolerance for dissent and of individual freedom and responsibility. They are willing to devote portions of their lives to voluntary work and may even plan their careers in such a way as to give prominence to social concerns. They tend to choose as leaders not men with an authoritarian style but those who are able to enlist them in a spirit of partnership around projects that have immediate practical consequences while serving a higher and well-articulated vision. They tend to conceive of their lives as a process not of material accumulation nor even of bureaucratic advancement but of learning, adventure and service."*

*Josiah Lee Auspitz*
*29-year-old President of the Ripon Society**

Reflecting on work stoppages by letter carriers and air traffic controllers, employees of the federal government, George P. Shultz, then Secretary of Labor, remarked:

*"Now we find we must be willing to change our view so that managers of public employees—at all levels—are no longer sovereigns who can't be challenged but managers who can."*

People don't want to follow the flag blindly. They want to know where it's going.

## 2.   WHAT'S WRONG WITH OUR ORGANIZATIONS?

If managers of venerable, slow-moving institutions are scampering to reform, they are doing so not because they are tender to criticism but because they know that they are failing to perform the job they chose as their own. Their systems are malfunctioning.

---

*   Excerpt from "For a Moderate Majority" by Josiah Lee Auspitz, reprinted by permission of *Playboy* magazine; copyright © 1970 by HMH Publishing Co. Inc.

Somehow the schools can't seem to teach. The mails grow more sluggish year by year. Transportation networks transport people slowly, not rapidly. Quality manufacturers produce shoddy wares. Recreational facilities fail to beguile. Police can't protect life and property, and welfare services don't seem to succor the helpless. And so on. Mighty organizations lose members and can't recruit replacements; meanwhile in the old membership the acid of resentment at stored-up grievances eats at the foundations of the existing order.

If we define a healthy organization as one that efficiently achieves its goals in a changing environment, then clearly many of our organizations are unwell.

What's wrong with them? What symptoms of malaise can be detected before abrupt collapse? What signs should the alert manager watch for and attempt to counteract lest he awaken one morning to find an ultimatum or a sheriff's padlock fastened to his door?

## 3. A SYMPTOMATOLOGY OF ORGANIZATIONAL ILLNESS AND HEALTH

In our view, a healthy organization is one that has a strong sense of its own identity and mission, yet has the capacity to adapt readily to change. Furthermore, we believe that a highly adaptive organization is most likely to search out and use the most effective methods for conducting its business.

Not included in this definition are other factors which may contribute to the organization's success, such as a favorable market or a particularly good information system. A market eager for its goods or services may enable an unhealthy organization to thrive for a long time—until a drop in demand exposes the organization's weaknesses.

Most organizations today typically exhibit behavior which would be characterized as immature or pathological in individuals. The most significant of these behavioral qualities seem to be the following.

### Dependency and Rebelliousness

The chiefs play at being powerful fathers; the Indians obey submissively or revolt or run away. This patriarchal enactment may be overt, as in most graduate schools, or subtly hidden, as in many sophisticated businesses. No one is really responsible for behaving toward an associate, a supervisor, or an employee in a grown-up way. The consequence is that people do not live up to their potential, nor do they pull their full weight.

### Defensiveness

We are not secure enough in ourselves, nor do we trust others enough, to let down our guard. The early implanted need to be perfect limits our capacity to learn from our own experience. Maskmanship and the N.I.H. ("Not Invented Here") factor limit our capacity to learn from others and to know and validate ourselves. We are crippled in our ability to grow; we stagnate.

### Narrowness of Perspective

We are unable to perceive what is happening in the world at large because we insist on peering through approved but narrow slits (traditional ways of looking at things). We therefore do not perceive our ever-changing situation afresh and in its totality, but in stylized ways. We respond to this subtotal vision with unrealistic, fragmented conduct. It is as if the coach of a last-place baseball team, noting his team's low batting average, sought to come out of the cellar only by improving batting strength. Thus we see the boss and not the man, and we act accordingly. We focus on the formal organization structure as if *that* were reality, not its underlying culture. We note formally allocated authority, not the real distribution of power and influence. We narrowly insist on the work necessary to complete the task and ignore the cross currents of activity motivated by personal needs. We see the organization as discrete, not complexly linked to its environment. The reality of the environment as a whole, which we willingly deny to our senses, constantly intrudes upon our oversimplified planning.

In any organization, the effect of everyday conduct conditioned by dependency and rebelliousness, defensiveness, and narrowness is a loss in "energy out." Instead energy is internally dissipated in frustration, protection of empires, sleep. People claw their way to the top of the heap at the expense of others and of the organization.

The healthy human being is independent, outgoing, optimistic, responsible for himself, not easily surprised, and responsive to change. We suggest that the healthy organization exhibits the same qualities. We have attempted to compare the attributes of healthy and unhealthy organizations in the table on pages 11–14.

The reader will recognize in the left column of the table the management culture and everyday behavior of a great many enterprises, perhaps most, with which he has come in contact. It is our belief that the longer those institutions resist change, the more likely they are to fall victim to the growing complexity of our civilization and the raised expectations of its population. Evidence that conventional methods of management will no longer work is provided by the mounting number of traditional organizations that are losing out.

During the last two decades, a new group of management theorists with strong roots in behavioral science have been pointing the way to organizational forms in which the manager maintains influence specifically by working *with* his employees instead of manipulating them (see the right column of the table). In most of the industrialized countries of the world there is awakening interest and substantial experimentation in human-centered and participative approaches to the governing of large industrial, educational, and state enterprises. Their leaders are attracted by advanced organizational forms because:

○ They believe that new kinds of organizations may be inherently more productive.

○ They feel they cannot afford the isolation of traditional office politics; they want all pertinent facts out in the open, not whispered in the hallways.

○ Those managers responsible for building or operating complex systems in which the parts of the system must speak to each other see the necessity of a climate in which the people who build and operate the system can freely speak to each other, too.

○ They see the possibility of working successfully with human beings who are as grown-up as they are, and they are enticed by the challenge.

SOME CHARACTERISTICS OF UNHEALTHY AND HEALTHY ORGANIZATIONS

**Unhealthy**

1. Little personal investment in organizational objectives except at top levels.

2. People in the organization see things going wrong and do nothing about it. Nobody volunteers. Mistakes and problems are habitually hidden or shelved. People talk about office troubles at home or in the halls, not with those involved.

3. Extraneous factors complicate problem-solving. Status and boxes on the organization chart are more important than solving the problem. There is an excessive concern with management as a customer, instead of the real customer. People treat each other in a formal and polite manner that masks issues —especially with the boss. Nonconformity is frowned upon.

4. People at the top try to control as many decisions as possible. They become bottlenecks, and make decisions with inadequate information and advice. People complain about managers' irrational decisions.

**Healthy\***

1. Objectives are widely shared by the members and there is a strong and consistent flow of energy toward those objectives.

2. People feel free to signal their awareness of difficulties because they expect the problems to be dealt with and they are optimistic that they can be solved.

3. Problem-solving is highly pragmatic. In attacking problems, people work informally and are not preoccupied with status, territory, or second-guessing "what higher management will think." The boss is frequently challenged. A great deal of nonconforming behavior is tolerated.

4. The points of decision-making are determined by such factors as ability, sense of responsibility, availability of information, work load, timing, and requirements for professional and management development. Organizational level as such is not considered a factor.

---

\*   The description of a healthy organization may appear millennialist. It is perhaps more a statement of direction than a state that has been achieved by any known organization.

SOME CHARACTERISTICS OF UNHEALTHY AND HEALTHY ORGANIZATIONS (Cont'd)

**Unhealthy**

5. Managers feel alone in trying to get things done. Somehow orders, policies, and procedures don't get carried out as intended.

6. The judgment of people lower down in the organization is not respected outside the narrow limits of their jobs.

7. Personal needs and feelings are side issues.

8. People compete when they need to collaborate. They are very jealous of their area of responsibility. Seeking or accepting help is felt to be a sign of weakness. Offering help is unthought of. They distrust each other's motives and speak poorly of one another; the manager tolerates this.

9. When there is a crisis, people withdraw or start blaming one another.

10. Conflict is mostly covert and managed by office politics and other games, or there are interminable and irreconcilable arguments.

11. Learning is difficult. People don't approach their peers to learn from them, but have to learn by

**Healthy**

5. There is a noticeable sense of team play in planning, in performance, and in discipline—in short, a sharing of responsibility.

6. The judgment of people lower down in the organization is respected.

7. The range of problems tackled includes personal needs and human relationships.

8. Collaboration is freely entered into. People readily request the help of others and are willing to give in turn. Ways of helping one another are highly developed. Individuals and groups compete with one another, but they do so fairly and in the direction of a shared goal.

9. When there is a crisis, the people quickly band together in work until the crisis departs.

10. Conflicts are considered important to decision-making and personal growth. They are dealt with effectively, in the open. People say what they want and expect others to do the same.

11. There is a great deal of on-the-job learning based on a willingness to give, seek, and use feedback and

SOME CHARACTERISTICS OF UNHEALTHY AND HEALTHY ORGANIZATIONS (Cont'd)

**Unhealthy**

their own mistakes; they reject the experience of others. They get little feedback on performance, and much of that is not helpful.

12. Feedback is avoided.

13. Relationships are contaminated by maskmanship and image building. People feel alone and lack concern for one another. There is an undercurrent of fear.

14. People feel locked into their jobs. They feel stale and bored but constrained by the need for security. Their behavior, for example in staff meetings, is listless and docile. It's not much fun. They get their kicks elsewhere.

15. The manager is a prescribing father to the organization.

16. The manager tightly controls small expenditures and demands excessive justification. He allows little freedom for making mistakes.

17. Minimizing risk has a very high value.

18. "One mistake and you're out."

**Healthy**

advice. People see themselves and others as capable of significant personal development and growth.

12. Joint critique of progress is routine.

13. Relationships are honest. People do care about one another and do not feel alone.

14. People are "turned on" and highly involved by choice. They are optimistic. The work place is important and fun (why not?).

15. Leadership is flexible, shifting in style and person to suit the situation.

16. There is a high degree of trust among people and a sense of freedom and mutual responsibility. People generally know what is important to the organization and what isn't.

17. Risk is accepted as a condition of growth and change.

18. "What can we learn from each mistake?"

SOME CHARACTERISTICS OF UNHEALTHY AND HEALTHY ORGANIZATIONS (Cont'd)

**Unhealthy**

**Healthy**

19. Poor performance is glossed over or handled arbitrarily.

19. Poor performance is confronted, and a joint resolution sought.

20. Organization structure, policies, and procedures encumber the organization. People take refuge in policies and procedures, and play games with organization structure.

20. Organization structure, procedures, and policies are fashioned to help people get the job done and to protect the long-term health of the organization, not to give each bureaucrat his due. They are also readily changed.

21. Tradition!

21. There is a sense of order, and yet a high rate of innovation. Old methods are questioned and often give way.

22. Innovation is not widespread but in the hands of a few.

22. The organization itself adapts swiftly to opportunities or other changes in its marketplace because every pair of eyes is watching and every head is anticipating the future.

23. People swallow their frustrations: "I can do nothing. It's *their* responsibility to save the ship."

23. Frustrations are the call to action. "It's my/our responsibility to save the ship."

There has been enough experimentation already to stimulate growing interest. The centers of the new management thought, in the U.S. and abroad, are entertaining visitors from all over the world, and new publications in the field are being disseminated to a growing audience of managers.

## 4.  ORGANIZATION DEVELOPMENT

In this book we emphasize two aspects of organization development*
(O.D.): (1) as a way of *managing change,* and (2) as a way of *focusing
human energy toward specific desired outcomes.* Our approach rests on
a fundamental belief that in any organizational setting the individual
members must have the opportunity to grow if an ailing organization is to revive or a vital one is to maintain its health.

*In managing change,* the methodology of O.D. is to work in
concert with the persons affected by the change.  Such methods
stimulate and foster "growing up" behavior in individuals.  Like-
wise, a chief characteristic of a grown-up is his ability to respond
creatively to problems or opportunities.  What is true of individuals
is true of the associations they form.

The essential feature of the O.D. methodology is first and fore-
most that it focuses on what is *practical;* that is, the most *practical*
approach to nearly any opportunity or problem involving two or more
persons requires that all persons act as if they are human beings, not
things or parts of human beings.  (Thus an accountant is a man or
woman skilled in accounting, not a computer or a role labeled "accountant" that is somehow dissociated from the person.)  And
conversely, when people work at the tasks involved in a change in
such a way that their humanness and entirety is engaged along with
other known factors, then they themselves recommence to grow.  To
be treated as an "it," so to treat yourself or others, is to be "busy
dying."  Besides, it's damned inefficient.  On the other hand, to treat
respectfully the person (including oneself) in any problem involving
persons is to be "busy being born."  Such problem-solving is a
remedy for problems and for man.

---

*    "O.D. is a response to change, a complex educational strategy intended
to change the beliefs, attitudes, values, and structure of organizations so that
they can better adapt to new technologies, markets, and challenges, and the
dizzying rate of change itself."  Warren G. Bennis, *Organization Development: Its Nature, Origins, and Prospects,* Addison-Wesley, Reading, Mass.,
1969.

Organization development is *a discipline for focusing human energy on specific goals.*   Most organizations begin purposively.   After a time, the goals of the group give way to individualistic aims and the institution begins to decay.

In a snapshot view, an ideal organization may resemble water gliding through a straight pipe; or it may look like rows of galley slaves stroking the sea hard and rhythmically; or like a man and his team ploughing a field.  The collective energy—of the separate drops of water, of the men and their oars, of the farmers, his beasts, and his plough—flows uniformly in one direction.

If we snap the shutter on an unhealthy organization, we get a very different picture of energy flow:

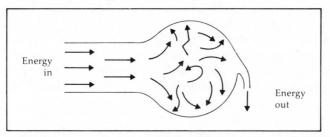

Here a tremendous amount of energy pours into the system at one end, but the real output dribbles out a pipette.  Most of the strength, talent, wisdom, force, liveliness, inventiveness, and joy of people is dissipated internally.

Organization development recognizes that all energy must be volunteered by the individual.  The wants and needs of the individual are therefore essential inputs to the goal-setting process of the group.  If each member participates in forming group goals and in general subscribes to those goals, then a considerable share of his energy, and the energy of his coworkers, begins to move toward a common purpose.

But we cannot expect a person to contribute creatively to a group's goal-setting process and invest his best energies unless the manager and the other members are willing to pay attention to his desires and to the way in which he customarily relates to the other members.

We might mention two misconceptions about organizational development that ought to be nailed.  One is that the process converts tough-minded managers into flabby, "be-nice-to-people" types. The truth is that a work culture of healthy confrontation can produce a tighter ship than Captain Bligh ever dreamed of.  That tough-minded gentleman is the prototype of an abysmally unsuccessful manager.

The second misconception about the O.D. approach is that it seeks the consensus of the group in all management decisions, and thus reduces the responsibility and force of the manager.  While O.D. methods do in fact frequently lead to consensus, the manager loses none of his final responsibility or authority.  In fact, the higher the mutual trust and openness in a group, the more freedom the manager has to act without fear of being misunderstood, and the more freedom he has to face the urgent demands of a situation, if necessary, in a unilateral manner.

## 5.  PLAN OF THIS BOOK

Experienced professional consultants in the field of organization development are often called Third Parties.  On the other hand, another manager—or indeed any impartial person—may on some occasions act for others in a Third Party capacity.  In many of the steps in the O.D. process, a Third Party is vital.  What his functions and qualifications are, and how you would select a suitable person for this role, are treated in the next section of Part One.

Part Two presents four case studies in which managers and their people embarked on jointly managed changes.  The cases have been selected not to illustrate large-scale change strategies, but to trace the day-by-day process of change accomplished by the methods described in Part Three.

Part Three, which forms the bulk of this volume, describes some 30 basic tools (plus variations) that are commonly employed in O.D. practice today and that have been tested in a wide range of institutional settings—including business, government, universities, the military, student groups, religious groups, interracial groups, etc.

A series of simple maps is presented in Part Three to outline typical routes that a manager and his organization may follow in an effort to produce change by O.D. methods. Some of the more complex methods are also flow-charted.

### 6. TO PROCEED

The manager who is discontent with the health of his organization and wishes to move toward management *with* people must recognize that an O.D. undertaking requires one basic condition: the persons involved must be willing to work jointly, at least to the point of engaging honestly with one another and not for an ulterior purpose. Given that condition, the manager may proceed by:

○ Working *with* the people who are affected by particular proposed changes in the organization.

○ *Linking* to all those who can influence the outcome.

○ Forming a tentative *general goal* which, by joint process, will convert to a specific group goal.

○ Working on *changing the quality of relationships* from one in which the individual is conditioned to isolation, destructive competition, and interpersonal conflict ("I'm up—you're down") to one of collaboration and healthy competition ("we"). To bring about such a change, the manager must encourage direct and open communication, and himself set an example.

○ Building active *feedback* loops from all knowledgeable sources so that he can perceive the shape of events as realistically as possible, and so as to monitor his organization's progress.

Like growing up, O.D. is continuous. There is no end state that we can imagine. We do believe that any organization that moves even a short distance toward organizational health (as described herein) gains new energy and capacity to initiate and respond to change.

# The Third Party

## 1. TWO TRADITIONS

*"We don't need outsiders butting into our business. We've had our differences before, and we've settled them all right. We'll settle this one between us in our own way."*

*"The third man in the ring is just as important as the champion and the challenger. If there's anything civilized about a boxing match, it's the presence of the referee."*

Two individuals or groups in dispute often want to deal directly with one another. The idea of seeking out a neutral intermediary may carry with it some hint of unmanly dependence.

On the other hand, we are accustomed to inviting arbiters in many contest situations or even where there is a possibility of dispute. Such persons are called referees, umpires, judges, trustees, mediators, counciliators, arbitrators, marriage counselors, etc. What we expect from them is impartiality and fairness to both parties. We are less sensitive about calling upon referees, more touchy about mediators and marriage counselors.

## 2. WHAT A THIRD PARTY DOES

The role of a Third Party in organization development is analogous to that of the above-mentioned officials, with two important differences.

The first major difference is that the Third Party is often introduced to the scene without a recognized set of rules to be invoked (unlike sports officials), and before there is a recognized dispute (unlike judges, mediators, marriage counselors, etc.). In a word, the Third Party in organization development is often called in by a group to help it explore its everyday conduct and to assist it in defining how it wishes to change and how it will go about making the change.

The second major difference in roles—and here the role of Third Party in organization development comes closest, say, to marriage counseling—is to guide the parties toward more self-sufficient behavior in solving their problems, not to make them dependent on him for decisions. In fact, he makes no decisions for anyone except himself.

Like skilled managers or other professionals, the trained Third Party (Organization Development Consultant) goes about his work without checklists. But if we were to make a short checklist of what he does, it might look something like this:

## 1. *Diagnosis*

Assist in diagnosing the current state of the organization in terms of its assumptions, values, internal and external relationships, power and influence, ways of dealing with conflict, distribution of energy, performance, market relations, ability to change, etc.

## 2. *Change Goals*

Aid in setting goals for change.

## 3. *Strategy*

Help in planning strategies for bringing about change.

## 4. *Tactics*

Aid in planning specific steps for pursuing the strategy (e.g., plan a team-building meeting, set up a critical meeting between two parties).

### 5. *Meeting Facilitating*

Monitor meetings and intervene when the group is moving slug-gishly. (Examples: Without being aware of it, the manager may dominate a meeting and prevent the free flow of conversation. Or rational progress on a problem may be delayed by emotionally held fortresses. The Third Party perceives the difficulties and helps the group to overcome them.)

### 6. *Risk-Taking*

Take the risk of saying what no one else feels free to say.

### 7. *Detachment*

By being impartial, encourage the group toward constructive action.

### 8. *Connection*

Tie together the parties to the problem. (Example: Encouraging managers with an interorganizational problem to get together.)

### 9. *Alternatives*

Introduce alternatives when conventional views of organizations and interpersonal relations blind participants to fresh possibilities.

### 10. *Forward Thrust*

Help monitor the change process and keep it moving strongly toward its strategic and tactical goals.


## 3.  QUALIFICATIONS OF A SKILLED THIRD PARTY

Since the Third Party consultant actively involves himself in the change process, his skills, and indeed his manner and style, are par-ticularly important.

He must understand change strategies and be inventive in adapt-ing them to the situation he is in.

He must be a highly sensitive listener and observer; he must understand and respond to the organization and its people, and not apply a standard "cure."

His language, personal qualities, and way of working must be acceptable to the organization he is seeking to help.

He needs the courage and independence to remain impartial, hold to an honest position, not sell out.

The skills he needs to facilitate confrontation are described by Walton*:

> *"The professional and personal qualities attributed to the third party which give the principals confidence in entering a confrontation and which facilitate confrontation processes include: (a) diagnostic skills, (b) behavioral skills in breaking impasses and interrupting repetitive interchange, (c) attitudes of acceptance, and (d) personal capacity to provide emotional support and reasurrance."*

### 4.   THE CLIENT AND THE THIRD PARTY

For the individual who serves as Third Party to be effective with his client, it is important that the two individuals feel comfortable enough with each other that they can develop a relationship in which there is free give-and-take.

The Third Party should take the lead in being candid so as to invite the frankness of the client. Moreover, the client must find the Third Party to be a discreet and trustworthy person. If the Third Party becomes a spy, a tool of the boss, a secret mastermind, he cannot serve effectively as an O.D. consultant.

### 5.   WHAT SORT OF THIRD PARTY HELP DO YOU NEED?

When you embark on a major change, you'll need a Third Party who is readily available to you. Probably you'll need at least one expe-

---

\*   Richard E. Walton, *Interpersonal Peacemaking: Confrontations and Third-Party Consultation,* Addison-Wesley, Reading, Mass., 1969.

rienced outside consultant whom you may pair with an inside person who understands O.D. or is actively learning about it.

For anyone who wishes to undertake a large change toward a healthy organization, an important part of this change strategy must be to develop a staff (specialists and managers) who can act as skilled Third Parties part- or full-time. Usually, the principal limiting factor to a major change is the shortage of such skills.

For a more detailed account of the use of Third Parties, see Chapter 10 of Richard Beckhard's *Organization Development: Strategies and Models.* How a Third Party works on the firing line is described by Edgar H. Schein in *Process Consultation: Its Role in Organization Development.*

# Part Two.   Four Case Studies

This part presents four quite different cases in which major organization development efforts were undertaken.

Case 1 describes reorganization of management functions in a five-state region of a retail chain. The goal of the effort was to increase profits sharply.

Case 2 is an account of a short-term drive to improve troubled relations between the project office of an aerospace company and its government customer. At stake were schedule slippages and cost overruns. In this example, organizations from two quite distinct work cultures sought to work through to each other in the midst of battle.

Case 3 presents the evolution of an innovative teacher education program at Immaculate Heart College, an institution in the midst of a sweeping transformation that included secularization of the faculty of teaching Sisters.

Case 4 outlines an effort to revitalize a 1000-man division of an engineering company. The initiative for the organization development work came from a newly hired divisional manager.

All four cases are based on actual recent experience and the descriptions reflect the real events in all major aspects as accurately as we know how.

The four cases illustrate the process of change in the context of organization development and the use of the methods presented in Part Three. We selected the cases for clarity and variety of illustration, not for success or failure of the effort. It would have been tidier (but less realistic) if each case had somehow drawn to a successful close. However, three of them are still in progress. The participants feel strongly that the manner in which they have directed their energies will contribute to the goals they have selected. In no sense do they feel "fixed" in good health any more than a person who pursues a short-term regimen of proper diet, rest, and exercise is certified thereafter as permanently well. Organization development, or the process of growing up organizationally, seems to them unending.

# Case 1.   Reorganization of a Retail Chain

A medium-term change effort (3 to 12 months)

STEPS

**I. Situation**

a) The district manager (D.M.) of a retail chain wants to increase profits substantially.

b) He sees the behavior of his staff, mostly merchandising specialists, as an obstacle and he wants to change their mode of operating. *They* want strong control over the store managers and the resolute backing of the D.M. *He* believes the store managers—he was once one himself—need greater autonomy and that the staff should accomplish more on their own before coming back to him with new demands for enforcement. The staff appears to him to be frustrated. Perhaps they think he's weak.

c) About half the time of the D.M. and staff is devoted to store inspections and the necessary travel between stores. These are intended to be helpful to the store managers. We don't know *their* opinion of the visits.

d) The D.M. has attended a headquarters team-building meeting and wants one for himself and his staff.

COMMENTS

I

This organization shows most of the symptoms of malaise listed on pages 11–14.

a) The D.M.'s goals are vague; he needs to make them specific and to buttress them with practical measures.

b) The D.M. has made a highly private assessment of the forces that aid and those that hinder him. He chooses the staff's method of operating as the key variable. His diagnosis of the situation is based on his own observation; he has not yet benefited by the perception of other eyes. The staff wants to shift the load to the D.M.

STEPS

COMMENTS

## II. Meeting of the D.M. with Third Party   (2 hours)

The D.M. describes his profit objectives and his diagnosis of the problem to the Third Party. They agree to consult the staff about a team-building meeting.

## III. Meeting of the D.M., Third Party, and District Staff at a Regular Staff Meeting   (1 hour)

The staff agrees to the team-building meeting.

## IV. Information Gathering (See Pages 140–142)   (1 hour per interview)

The Third Party interviews staff members individually about the changes they want, and how they and the D.M. function as a team.

## V. Team-building Meeting with D.M. and Staff   (2½ days)

a) The D.M. invites the staff to air their complaints. They do, and there are three: (1) the D.M. won't

II

The D.M. takes the critical step of seeking help.

III

Working together starts here.

IV

Working together requires getting everyone's information out on the table. This is not as simple as it appears. We are not as outspoken as we pretend to be.

*"We do not agree, really, on very much, because we do not propose to confess very much about what is going on in our heads."*

*David Cort*

Interviewing is one way to start. Others are described in Part Three.

V

a) This is the "garbage out" process characteristic of team-building meetings. As their personal con-

STEPS

back their directives to store managers, (2) he won't close down un-
profitable stores, and (3) he won't
fire incompetent store managers in
spite of the staff's repeated recommendations. In short, in their view,
he *is* a weak and indecisive leader!
After considerable discussion, the
D.M. now consents to some of their
recommendations. On others they
compromise. The D.M. now feeds
back to the staff *his* dissatisfaction
with their way of operating.

b) Following more work on their
desires and relationships, the team
develops a "turned-on" feeling.
The staff members now want to include the store managers in their
team.

c) The D.M. formally announces an
ambitious profit goal.

COMMENTS

cerns are dealt with, people in the
group feel relieved and anxious to
turn their energies toward the group's
goals. The process is cathartic, in
effect, but it also leads to other
changes that need to be made. It is
a pooling of views which more
brightly illuminates the situation.
In this case, for instance, the manager started by assuming that the
major problem was that the staff
didn't understand its role. But
their frustration with him points to
another difficulty that he begins to
grasp: sometimes he *is* indecisive.

b) A new experience opens the
eyes of the staff to other ways of
dealing with their relations with the
store managers. Escaping the limits
of conventional solutions is a primary objective of O.D.

c) The announcement of a specific
dollar goal at this point serves as a
major stimulus to the group. However, at this point the goal is still a
dream. It is interesting to note that,
early in the meeting, the members
frequently (and truculently) insist
that their only reason for being is
*profit*. By the end of the meeting
there is a shift in emphasis: profit is
a measure of themselves as a team.

STEPS

d) After much analysis and debate, they agree to the D.M.'s goal and draw up a list of the steps needed to reach it.  Three of these are particularly significant:

○ Recognizing that achievement of this goal requires the same commitment from the store managers as *they* now feel, as well as close teamwork between them, they recommend that the D.M. conduct a similar meeting with store managers, followed by a joint meeting of store managers and staff.

○ They realize that they have been acting as policemen to the stores, a role they now want to cast off. They want to change the nature of their store inspections to allow for more healthy give-and-take between the store managers and themselves.

○ They introduce an innovation. They will invite a representative group of store managers to take part in developing this year's standards of performance for store managers.

**VI. Visits of the Third Party to Several Ensuing Biweekly Meetings of the D.M. and Staff  (1 day each)**

The Third Party consults with the group on its progress.  In each case

COMMENTS

d) They begin to plan ways to link the people instrumental to the change.  They now have higher standards for the closeness of these linkages (relationships).  These are fundamental concepts of O.D.

VI

Par for the course.  Nothing ever stays fixed.  After several expe-

STEPS

there are fresh difficulties: unforeseen factors have appeared and new issues have arisen between them that they did not openly confront. Some feel that the manager or certain staff members are backsliding on commitments. These problems are finally confronted and resolved.

COMMENTS

riences, the group members learn in their hearts what they already knew in their heads: that no one can change his characteristic behavior without repeated reinforcement, that neither the D.M. nor any other single person alone can carry the responsibility for meeting all the commitments made. Each has to assume responsibility for helping the others stay honest.

**VII. Meeting Between D.M., the Staff, Four Store Managers, and the Third Party   (1½ days)**

This is the meeting on standards of performance recommended by the staff at their team-building meeting.

**VII**

This meeting also serves as a means of bridging to the store manager group. The store managers invited were all outspoken people and highly respected by their peers. They jointly decide in the meeting that the store managers should not act as "shills" within their own group, but should feel free to discuss any aspect of the meeting according to their own judgment. (When working *with* people, don't contaminate the process by working *on* them.)

a) The four store managers are briefed on the earlier meeting and the new profit goal. They debate the new goal.

STEPS

b) The store managers agree that, to achieve the goal, standards of performance must be given more weight, and the relationship between the staff and the store managers must change.

c) The store managers seriously question the usefulness of store inspections; the D.M. agrees to improve them, but not to reduce frequency.

## VIII. Team-building Meeting with the D.M., Store Managers, and Third Party   (2½ days)

a) The D.M. sets the stage for this meeting by inviting the store managers to get their problems off their chests, including the problems with *him,* and by stating that they are there to tear apart their whole pattern of working and put it back together again in a better way.  All his earlier decisions are subject to question, and he is prepared to fight the battle higher up if necessary.

b) As in the staff team-building meeting, when issues and feelings are ventilated, the group experiences a sense of unity.

COMMENTS

b) The goal grows more real as personal risks intensify.  In turn, this focuses attention on the need for improved ways of helping one another.

c) The D.M. still does not feel free to "let go."

## VIII

a) By this time, the manager clearly realizes that he is and wants to be involved in a major change process. In his own way, he states clearly the process of change in a human system: a period of unfreezing the old system, exploring and deciding on new ways, and refreezing.

As he and the group unlock from the old system, their horizons broaden, and they experience a feeling of increased power to determine their own destiny.  They will tangle with headquarters, if necessary!

b) The scene grows clearer.  Without exception, each of the store managers reveals himself as strongly motivated to do a better job, al-

STEPS

COMMENTS

though many of them previously felt themselves hobbled by a need to protect themselves from the staff. They had been harassed by policemen and judged by judges, whereas what they had needed was people who could help them. Now, when they see the real possibility of remaking their business world into one of their own choice, they are understandably excited.

c) They explore ways in which there could be more help in merchandising methods from the staff, other store managers, or experienced department managers (within each store).

c) They are starting to design the new world.

d) Their solution to the problem with the staff (the hottest issue) is to make the staff *jointly* responsible with them for the effectiveness of merchandising in their stores. Only the D.M. is the policeman; his principal means of control will be a quarterly review of store managers' performance against their annual standards.

d) Creative solution.

e) The D.M. isn't ready to reply to either this recommendation or the one on store inspections, but carries them over until the intergroup meeting between the store managers and the staff.

e) The D.M. learns that he is in a period of exploration when withholding decisions does not signify indecisiveness. On the other hand, he still needs to make his views known, with the understanding that they are tentative. The give-

STEPS

COMMENTS

and-take has made the group members confident enough that he can speak freely without inhibiting them.

**IX**

**IX**

The D.M. makes a five-state tour during which he meets individually with each store manager to negotiate the store manager's performance standards for the year. The staff no longer takes part in setting standards for store managers.

The increase in trust makes these negotiations more realistic.

**X. Intergroup Team-building Meeting Between the Staff and the Store Managers, with the D.M. and Third Party** (2½ days)

**X**

a) Each group presents the other with its complaints.

a) "Garbage out" again. Not many surprises this time.

b) The store managers present their solution:

b)

○ The staff should have less close relations with the D.M. and instead should associate with them, taking equal rights and responsibilities.

This recommendation has earth-shaking implications. For the staff it means a departure from the organization chart box at the D.M.'s level, with an implication of loss of status and power. But the staff is now disenchanted with that role. They see themselves having more real influence by working *with* the store managers, with no distinction in rank. For the store managers, this recommendation means trusting the staff enough to give them

STEPS

COMMENTS

complete access to their stores. For both of them, it means being willing to fight out issues between them. For the D.M., it means apparent isolation. The staff can no longer serve as his intelligence agents or help him make decisions about store managers. But he trusts their commitment to work responsibly. The strengthened personal bonds mitigate his feeling of isolation.

○ The store managers, in like manner, will work jointly with their department (e.g., sporting goods) managers in the stores.

After a good deal of probing and soul-searching, this concept is approved and bought by all, including the D.M.

c) In round-robin nose-to-nose confrontations, working in small groups, store managers and staff members disclose what they like and don't like about their past relations and how they want to frame a new contract.

c) They are further strengthening relations and starting to work out details.

d) The D.M. agrees that there will be *no more routine inspections,* and that when inspections are necessary, the inspecting group may include other store managers but will *not* include the staff (since they would now also be implicated in any cases

d) A new trust and the new ways of working reduce the D.M.'s dependence on these traditional controls so that he can let go. This means bucking the system, because regular inspections are company standard practice. The D.M. had

STEPS

of poor performance).  In future, the purpose of inspection will be to solve problems, not to trap "delinquents."

e) They agree that any store manager may at any time request a task force of his choice to help him, including other store managers and store department managers.

f) They decide that their quarterly performance reviews with the D.M. should be conducted *in the total group,* so they can learn from one another, help one another, and maintain group discipline!  These same meetings will also be used to formulate critiques of their progress as a team.  They decide to *invite the vice-president* to these meetings!

### XI.  Situation as of Today

The basic change in the situation occurred in about four months.  In effect, the change in relationships makes it possible to shift a large

COMMENTS

already paved the way for this by keeping the vice-president informed of what he was doing. (Never overlook links with more powerful levels of management.)

e) The culture is changing from isolation, defensiveness, and destructive competition to one of open competition with collaboration, which the participants now see as to their mutual benefit and personal satisfaction.

f) Here is testimony to their increased level of confidence!  This is a creative and highly important decision.  It accomplishes two things, both basic to change by O.D. methods.  First, the total group assumes responsibility for the change and its management.  Group collaboration and discipline replaces inefficient management controls. Second, a routine mechanism for periodic *"critiquing"* is built in.  In O.D., periodic group "critiquing" is a basic method for maintaining forward thrust and adjusting the direction of thrust.

### XI

Refer to the table on pages 11–14. This organization in four months has moved a long way from ill health toward good health.  A num-

STEPS

amount of energy and talent from policing, attack and defense, and plain idleness to mutual help. Management energy now flows in the same direction.

One significant characteristic of the management team after these events is that it has developed a fair amount of sophistication about how it got there and what it has to do to keep going. The members of the team have developed a code to warn one another of backsliding. Backsliding means:

○ Not confronting issues.

○ Not listening to one another.

○ Not living up to commitments.

○ Trying to do things *to*, rather than *with*, one another.

COMMENTS

ber of threads, common to O.D. change efforts, run through this process.

The manager of such a change needs, above all else, courage and persistence. He needs the strength to listen to accounts of his real and imagined defects without counter-attacking, to risk experimenting with ways of "running the railroad" which are not generally understood and accepted, and to deal with his boss or other power figures when the need arises. He needs persis-tence, in the face of competing de-mands for resources and his time, to carry through the change process and make it stick. It takes a lot of energy and it costs money to execute a major change.

# Summary Observations

This case highlights some fundamental emphases in O.D.

*Goal Setting*

The realism of goals depends on our real commitment to them. The elements of real commitment are: that the boss himself means it and is willing to stick his neck out; that the goal is thoroughly discussed and understood by all; and that the conditions of its attainment (means, standards, rewards, risks, and help) are understood and widely subscribed to as illustrated in this example. This is a complex process which depends for its success on confrontation and frank discussion, not wishful thinking or saluting the flag.

*Understanding the Situation*

Change by O.D. methods requires that the understanding be a joint one and that it include mature understanding of feelings and personal needs that influence behavior. Sharing of this type of information is gradual, based on evolving trust, which in turn is based on willingness to express feelings and desires.

*Improving Relations*

Improvements in relations are a continuous by-product of change by O.D. methods. The means are simple in concept: bring to the surface both the issues and the positive feelings between people.

As this happens, they begin to value more the satisfaction they can get from working together.  Materialism is less important.

*Working With the Forces in the Situation*

Kurt Lewin, whose work in group dynamics underlies organization development practice, pointed out that change in a human system depends on the balance of forces within it.  So if you are interested in a particular change, it is useful to make an inventory of the forces going your way and those opposing.  We do this instinctively, but we can also open new possibilities by being more systematic.  A method for doing this is explained on pages 106–108.  One thing Lewin observed is that resistance to change can be dealt with by two methods: (1) by building up pressure against the resistance, or (2) by reducing the resistance.  The problem he found with building up pressure (as with orders and exhortation) is that there is a tendency for the force of resistance to mount in response; and even though the change may come about, the forcing method takes more energy and leaves a residue of ill will.  (A common illustration in groups is the phenomenon of members verbally beating on someone to change his behavior.  The result is intensification of conflict.)  Reducing resistance to change is usually more successful.  The most effective way Lewin found for reducing resistance to change was through participative group work.

In the example of the retail chain, the D.M.'s appraisal of the forces in his situation was that he could produce the biggest increment of positive change by altering the relationship of the staff to the store managers to a more collaborative one.  We share his diagnosis.  In our opinion, the original staff solution—building up pressure on the store managers—would have magnified the conflict.

*Linking*

A fundamental strategy of organization development is to link people who are significant forces in the change. Team-building is a way of linking people strongly.  Not all links need to be that strong.  In the example, the D.M. has established minimal links with his boss.  Inviting him to the quarterly performance review meetings would involve him more, hopefully in a mutually helpful manner. Steps had also been taken to form tighter connections with the head-quarters staff, and some store managers were starting to work on strengthening relations within their own stores. It is impossible to change one part of a human system without affecting other parts. If the other parts are unhealthy, they may arrest growth in the developing parts. On the other hand, the beneficent influence of growth in one part of an organization can readily be felt in others, as in the instance of the individual retail stores' internal organizations.

# Case 2.   A Problem of Customer Relations in an Aerospace Firm

A short-term change (less than 3 months)

STEPS

COMMENTS

## I. Situation

I

a) An aerospace contractor is in trouble on a project. The cost-plus contract is overrunning its budget. Technical problems are delaying the schedule.

b) Relations between the project people and the customer's representatives have deteriorated. A distressing amount of time is lost in coping with increasingly frantic pressure from the customer. The customer representatives complain more and more loudly that the project team is withholding information and is behaving dishonestly. Certain individuals from each side have become so antagonistic that they refuse to speak to one another.

b) Diagnosis: Clear case of organization ill health. In this case, the parties in the dispute are two organizations which do not belong to a single larger organization and which manifest different work cultures. This situation naturally invites interorganizational conflict, especially when the relationship is weakened by a work crisis. Special attention is required.

## II. Meetings Between the Project Manager, the Customer's Executives, and a Third Party (Two major meetings, 2 hours each)

II

a) The project manager calls this meeting to discuss the unsatisfactory relationship between the two groups. While this has been a frequent topic of conversation in the past, he now proposes an Intergroup Team-building Meeting (see pages 124–130) as a fresh approach to the problem.

a), b), c) Differences in work culture, role, and organization membership are disuniting forces which offset the positive force of a common desire to get the job done. The customer executive is concerned that entering into a form of team-building with a contractor might compromise his independent role as

STEPS

b) The project manager is familiar with this method from past experience. What is new to him is the idea of attempting it with persons outside the company. This suggestion came from the Third Party, with whom he had worked before.

c) The customer executive is concerned about the negative implications of such a meeting. He feels that developing closer personal ties between his staff and the contractor's project team will interfere with their official objectivity. Scenting the possibility of seduction, he forcefully rejects the proposal.

d) During the next few months, the project manager brings up the same suggestion each time there is a new explosion between the groups. The customer executive finally agrees to risk the meeting.

e) His decision leads to a second meeting with the Third Party during which they plan and schedule the intergroup meeting.

**III. Intergroup Team-building Meeting of the Project Management Group, the Customer Group, Both Managers, and the Third Party (15 people)   (1½ days)**

a) The managers state their joint objective of laying the cards on the

COMMENTS

customer. The project manager certainly doesn't want to offend his customer. However, the project manager's corporate culture encourages him to enter into such a meeting, while the customer's organizational culture does not. Their separate work experiences have instilled in them different standards and different levels of optimism about teamwork. Recognizing this disparity, the Third Party raises these issues for discussion in the first meeting.

d) Most people don't risk new solutions until they're really suffering. A sense of risk is a normal feature of O.D. work. Nothing ventured, nothing gained.

**III**

a) The managers take the first step and set the example.

STEPS

table and improving working relationships.

b) The Third Party explains the meeting procedure in detail.

c) Each group goes off by itself to prepare three lists: (1) whatever it is the group thinks the other group does well, if anything, (2) actions and attitudes of the other group that make matters worse, of which there is evidently an abundance, and (3) what the group predicts the other group will have on its lists.

The groups reassemble and each presents its lists to the other. An agenda is established. The issues are dealt with and action items agreed upon.*

COMMENTS

b) No surprises, please! Everyone's nervous as it is.

c) Each group starts with the positive side of things; this makes it possible to keep the negative in perspective. Don't underrate the positive! In this case, the accumulated load of negatives is heavy. There is an uproar. The air is filled with charges and countercharges of arrogance, untrustworthiness, ignorance, incompetence, and habitual concealment of blunders. People walk out of the room in high dudgeon. That's all in the day's work for the Third Party, who recognizes that, when people are learning new ways of relating, he must provide some sort of firm structure. The meeting plan and his presence do this. He also reminds them of the futility of casting abstract charges, such as, "I think you're concealing mistakes." The grievance must be reduced to specifics: "This is what you did that makes me think you are concealing mistakes."

---

* For an explanation of this procedure, see page 125.

STEPS

d) The following results are achieved:

○ Each side comes to understand better the way the other group functions, so that misunderstandings are less likely and each group can adjust somewhat to the other's needs.

○ Better means for reporting and communication are worked out.

○ Unsolved technical problems, contract changes, and management problems are identified and joint task groups are formed to work on them.

○ Arrangements are made for persons who are extremely hostile to one another to meet separately with the Third Party.

Two subsequent meetings are agreed upon, one two weeks later to deal with the recommendations of the joint task groups, and one six weeks later to review the relationships at that point.

○ Plans are made for reporting the results of the meeting to others in the respective organizations.

COMMENTS

○ Good planning.

○ Again, note the importance of linking to those affected by the change. This was particularly important in this case to avoid suspicion that the contractor and customer representatives at the meeting were in collusion.

STEPS

**IV. Meeting of the Same Group to Act on the Task Group Recommendations   (4 hours)**

**V. Meeting of the Same Group Six Weeks Later to Review Relations   (1 day)**

THIS MEETING IS NOT HELD.

**VI. Situation**

a) Nevertheless, relations are greatly improved. The groups feel better about themselves and each other.

b) The honeymoon lasts several months. Then the relationships start to deteriorate seriously. However, the project is nearly completed.

c) However, because the customer had, for a period at least, stopped breathing down their necks, the members of the project team were able to put all their energy into getting the job done more effectively.

d) They had also learned a method of improving relations that they could use in the future, and they had come to understand better the customer and contractor roles and problems.

COMMENTS

**IV.** Good follow-through.

**V**

Why bother? Things aren't bad and we don't have time.

**VI**

b) Sad and predictable. Compare with Case 1, in which the participants put great effort into learning and relearning by experience how to maintain team relations.

# Summary Observations

This case illustrates the use of one of the methods described in Part Three (the Intergroup Team-building Meeting) to solve a specific management problem. The methods can be used in this *ad hoc* manner, but the chances of their being used, and used successfully, are greatly increased if they are part of an overall continuing change strategy. In this case it would have been simpler to get started if the customer had had an O.D. program of his own, and there would have been greater likelihood of follow-up.

The Intergroup Team-building Meeting generally takes place within an organization, but it has wider utility. For example, it has been used in groups of mixed ages to bridge the generation gap, and it has been successfully applied in families to reconcile differences between husband and wife and between parents and children.

# *Case 3.   The Development of a Teacher Education Program*

An open-ended evolutionary change

STEPS*

## I. Situation

a) Immaculate Heart College (IHC) is a small liberal arts college in Los Angeles. The college drew national attention as the home of the artist Sister Mary Corita. It was also the scene of a widely-reported disagreement between the Sisters of the Immaculate Heart and Cardinal McIntyre of Los Angeles over their desire to enter upon an exploratory mode of living which included freedom to wear civilian dress. The order recently made the decision to withdraw from official canonical status as Sisters while continuing as a community. The college was undergoing other changes, including a planned move of the physical campus 40 miles east to Pomona to join a small complex of high-quality institutions known as the Claremont Colleges.

This case concerns a change in teacher education at IHC. California state law with respect to teacher credentials requires that the teacher major in an academic disci-

COMMENTS

## I

a) A change in conditions (moving to Pomona) makes a decision necessary (whether or not to give up teacher education).

---

* We are indebted for the information for this case study to Dr. Veronica Flynn, the Coordinator of Teacher Education (CTE) in the study. Dr. Flynn is a trained Third Party; however, the comments are our own.

STEPS

COMMENTS

pline—i.e., not in education—for
undergraduate study. Thirty hours
beyond the B.A. are required in
addition. IHC accordingly offered a graduate program in teacher
education. Since the Claremont
Graduate School, serving all the colleges, now has such a program, IHC
decided to drop its own program
upon moving to Pomona.

b) Meanwhile, the college's Liberal
Arts Study Committee recommended the liberalization of undergraduate course requirements.
Within the context of major
and minor courses of study, each
student was to take substantial responsibility for his curriculum, se-
lecting courses of study appropriate
to his interests and goals. This
movement was successful at IHC
and is now in effect. The school
is truly in a ferment of change.

c) The liberalization of the curriculum unlocked many closed doors.
Behind one such door lay the subject of teacher education, which
IHC had just decided to drop as a
postgraduate program. Now the
subject was looked at freshly. A
consequence was that the Dean of
the School of Education (DSE) and
the Coordinator of Teacher Education (CTE) set a general goal, with

c) Freeing up the culture stimulates
innovation. (Note the similarity to
Case 1.)

STEPS

the approval of the college president, to develop an undergraduate program in teacher education which students can follow as electives.

d) This program has three primary objectives:

○ To be available to any student as electives in education.

○ To give the individual student freedom to form his own program, following his own natural learning process.

○ To be a campus-wide program, "owned" by all the departments.

COMMENTS

d) This change process is enormously strengthened by the school's consistency in carrying out its basic beliefs. It is not saying one thing and doing something else. There is a widespread belief at Immaculate Heart College that the process of learning is highly variable among individuals and individually determined. The college sees learning as a process in which the learner takes a step, assesses his new situation, selects new steps, and so on.

Because the student is not always able to make the assessment and see new steps entirely on his own, IHC emphasizes feedback, critique, help, and counseling—in short, change by joint action. There is also an emphasis on the unfolding of new goals as opposed to their predetermination. This approach is ideally suited to exploration of unknown territory. Here the IHC view of learning is applied consistently— to practice teaching, to the education of the teacher herself, to the unfolding of the teacher education program, and to the development of campus-wide joint "ownership."

STEPS

COMMENTS

Joint ownership was selected over School of Education ownership to promote the integration of teacher education with the rest of the college. [Joint ownership and cross-fertilization are prescriptions for bureaucratic isolation. For methods, see the discussions of the Organization Mirror (pages 101–105) and the Intergroup Team-building Meeting (pages 124–130).]

## II. Assessment Activities   (During a 2-month period)

The DSE and CTE meet with other faculty and students representing all departments for a mutual exploration of views on teacher education in general and what might be desirable and feasible specifically at IHC.

**II**

The main purpose of this process is to assess the forces for and against a given change objective (see Force Field Analysis, pages 106–108). This assessment helps to shape the objective so that it is practical and attainable. It also helps to identify and establish links with persons who can act as positive forces for change —in short, those with interest, energy, and time.

## III. Broadening the Base   (School term)

a) The CTE joins a group of seven faculty members involved in an experimental interdisciplinary seminar in Identity and Discovery funded by the Danforth Foundation.

**III**

a) Linking to ideas.  Under terms of the Danforth grant, which recognized the program as "the seed of a genuinely revolutionary approach to the undergraduate curriculum," a group of faculty members are

STEPS

COMMENTS

given reduced course loads each term to plan and conduct two interdisciplinary seminars, aimed at seeking "the integration of knowledge by capitalizing on the specialization which is a hallmark of our age." Departments receive grant funds for replacement of faculty involved in the seminars and to test new ideas stirred up in the campuswide reflection on education.

b) The CTE asks this group to join with her to explore the significance of the Danforth seminars for teacher education. They agree to work on the problem during their regular weekly meetings during the term.

b) Linking with activists.

c) One of the Danforth faculty, a member of the Economics Department, becomes so interested that she volunteers to be cochairwoman with the CTE of the new teacher education program.

c) Linking with the academic departments.

d) The Academic Dean is invited to join the group and does so.

d) Linking with authority.

e) The group prepares a preliminary proposal for the new teacher education program and presents it at a faculty meeting, along with a general invitation to a weekend planning conference.

e) The new program has now become a true group effort, cutting across academic disciplines.

| STEPS | COMMENTS |
|---|---|
| **IV. Planning the Weekend Planning Conference** (**During a 5-week period**) | IV |
| a) The cochairwomen (the CTE and the faculty member from the economics department) carry out meetings and related activities to prepare for the conference. | |
| b) Two Third Parties help in the planning. | b) Linking to experts in the process of change. |
| **V. The Weekend Planning Conference** (**Friday evening and Saturday**) | V |
| *Friday Evening* | |
| a) Two speakers address an audience of several hundred people. The keynote speaker is nationally known as a leader of change in the field of education. The other speaker is local and respected in the college. Both present fresh ideas about education. | a) The stimulus of new ideas from respected sources. |
| b) The audience is made up of students, faculty, and administrators of the college, *plus* public and private school superintendents, teachers, and principals from the area. | b) Linking with the internal and external communities interested in education. |
| *Saturday* | |
| c) Over a hundred volunteers from the Friday evening audience meet. | c) Self-selection of those with enough interest to contribute to the next step. |

STEPS

(This excludes all outsiders except those with specific invitations.)

d) There is a general discussion followed by discussions in small subgroups. The subgroups record on large sheets of paper their views on ideas and values that should be incorporated in the new teacher education program. Spokesmen for each subgroup report their results to the larger group.

## VI. Critique and Planning Meetings (Two meetings, several hours each)

a) The cochairwomen meet to evaluate the conference, classify the information obtained from it, consider its implications, and plan the next steps. In this process they confer with the two Third Parties.

b) A report on the conference, including the information as classified, is sent to all conferees, with an invitation to maintain two-way communication.

c) The cochairwomen decide that they should now involve the cre-

COMMENTS

d) Subgrouping is a way to get more involvement by individuals, and to work through ideas and make them more specific. (See Subgrouping, pages 162–165; and Chart Pads, pages 157–159.) It facilitates this process, helps in reporting back to the larger group, and becomes a record for summarizing meeting results for the next step.

VI

a) This is part of the unfolding process of change. At each major step there is a critique of past action and a determination of the next. In this, Third Parties, who are not involved in the action, can be helpful.

b) We like to know the results of our efforts, and to know we can continue to influence the process. Throughout this change, the conferees, the faculty, the college community in general, and interested outsiders are informed at each major step. Knowing that something is really happening awakens interest.

c) Linking with external formal authority.

STEPS

COMMENTS

dentialing authority of the State
Board of Education in view of the
fact that they are proposing to complete all teacher education in the
undergraduate school.

### VII. Meetings of Planning Task Group  (Two meetings, several hours each)

**VII**

a) A planning group is made up of
46 volunteers from the conference,
including faculty, students, and outside educators.

a) Here is another instance of self-
selection of those with enough interest to spend more time.  This
was a larger group than needed,
but the wide interest was wel-
comed and used to form the planning group.  This is an example of
letting the structure evolve.

b) Drawing on ideas from the conference, this group develops long-
and short-range goals for the new
program and general educational
objectives for students and faculty
in the program.  The goals and objectives include both *program goals,*
such as working with the public
schools to develop experimental
learning environments, and *attitude
goals,* such as viewing learning as a
source of joy and a means of facilitating personal development and
freedom.

b) The goals are getting more specific and better understood.

c) The group sets up a Steering
Committee of 10 members with
decision-making responsibility for

c) A group of 46 is felt to be cum-
bersome as the planning gets more
specific.  The group solves this
problem to its satisfaction.

STEPS

COMMENTS

working out detailed implementation of the program.  This is done
by consensus.  The Steering Committee includes the DSE, the cochairwomen, four students from
different departments, a faculty
member from the Foreign Language
Department, the Academic Dean,
and a Supervisor of the Los Angeles City School District.  The
Steering Committee is to report
progress to the Planning Task Group
and reunite with it on major issues.

**VIII.  Steering Committee Meet-
ings   (Several, from a few hours
to a full day)**

**VIII**

At these meetings, the Steering
Committee makes the following decisions:

a) To offer a pilot, experimental
course called "Explorations in
Learning," to be open to all students, from freshmen to seniors,
who want to explore the process of
learning, whether or not they have
decided to become teachers.  The
course is to provide an opportunity
for students to observe their *own*
learning processes and those of students in a variety of elementary and
secondary schools, with an eye
toward formulating their own goals.

a) The change begins to broaden
out to affect the concepts of learning in the total college community.
Note the consistency with which
the college's views on learning are
applied.  See Comment I(d) above.

STEPS

b) To continue to involve public and private school teachers, supervisors, and administrators in the development of the program.

c) To communicate with other publics, e.g., parents and representatives of the Taxpayers Association.

d) To invite the college faculty to participate in the program in two ways: (1) by giving teaching time and (2) by planning and providing courses specifically for learning in their fields.

e) To follow an "action research model"* in developing the program.

COMMENTS

b) The teachers, supervisors, and administrators are aware of the tough, day-to-day realities of operating educational institutions; their support is needed; they too can learn.

c) Help or hindrance can come from many sources, and their learning needs to start now too. A lot of people don't like to have *faits accomplis* sprung on them.

d) The Steering Committee is reaching out for total faculty involvement and the use of the many resources available in the different departments. Note that this also encourages faculty members to criticize the ideas and methods of learning in their own specialties.

e) The "action research model" is implicit in the college's views on learning as discussed in Comment I(d) above. It is an unfolding process of learning and change. Instead of trying to predetermine a series of steps in detail, the participants evaluate each step before deciding on and taking the next step. Each step is seen as having the potential for opening new horizons, or revealing that the step

---

*    See Newton Margulies and Anthony P. Raia, "Action Research and the Consultative Process," *Business Perspectives*, Fall 1968, pp. 26–30.

STEPS

COMMENTS

selected was the wrong one. In this case, for example, the students and faculty involved in the course "Exploration in Learning" will evaluate that course before deciding on the next step.

f) To refer to the Planning Task Group the question of counseling for students interested in teaching.

f) With the emphasis on self-determination by students, the character of guidance to them is a major issue.

## IX. Situation as of Today

At this point, a year and a half after the initial decision to drop teacher education at Immaculate Heart, the course "Exploration in Learning" has been given and is in the process of evaluation. It appears to be highly successful. Many members of the faculty have responded positively to the invitation for their involvement. A number of departments are preparing courses focusing on the process of learning in their fields. The entire college community is aware of what is going on. Teacher education, once to be abandoned, has become an important and growing stimulus to the entire college, reaching out beyond the bounds of teacher education to the whole issue of learning.

# *Summary Observations*

This case illustrates four key points about change by O.D. methods.

*I. Linking*

In the change process described, appropriate links are established to those who have ideas or specialized knowledge, who can provide a stimulus, who can provide a link to others, who can and will do some of the work, who have authority or influence, who are affected by the change, whose support is required, and who can provide feedback.

"Appropriate" linkings are determined by the importance of involving a given person or group at a particular point in the change. For example, the linking process in this case followed a definite pattern, as illustrated at the top of page 63.

Phase I is a period of increasingly wide involvement, fitting the functions to be performed:

○ Assessment of the situation.

○ "Preparing the soil" by the infusion and exchange of ideas.

○ Locating and organizing "activists."

Phase II is a planning period, with decreasing involvement, appropriate to moving from a condition of general goals and ideas to specific plans and decisions.

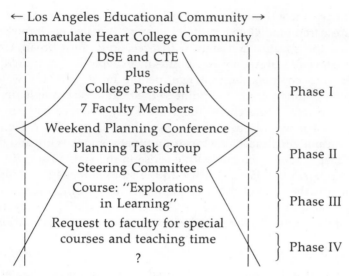

← Los Angeles Educational Community →
Immaculate Heart College Community

DSE and CTE
plus
College President
7 Faculty Members
Weekend Planning Conference          Phase I

Planning Task Group                  Phase II
Steering Committee

Course: "Explorations
in Learning"                         Phase III

Request to faculty for special
courses and teaching time            Phase IV
?

Phase III is an action period, starting with a specific action (the course "Explorations in Learning") and moving out to involve the total college community.

Phase IV is a continuing action research period, now starting, in which each action taken is evaluated and new steps decided upon, with no prescribed end state. Linking in this period will be primarily with those who are interested in getting into the action, but keeping the total community informed. This strategy generally results in a broadening of involvement.

Linking is something we all do to get what we want. In O.D. there is a special effort to ensure that these links are open and aboveboard, not manipulative. They also receive systematic attention, which helps to overcome the hazards of masterminding. We repeat that extensive linking (as illustrated here) is not appropriate to many changes. Frequently a quick one-man decision makes sense.

*II. The Unfolding Character of Change in Organizations*

This has been referred to above in comments on the prevalent views at Immaculate Heart about the process of learning. These views are deliberately incorporated in Phase IV by the decision to use the action research model. In a complex change, it is usually impossible to define the specific end state with precision. In a broad sense, there are no end states, only way points in an evolutionary unfolding. Further, in a complex joint change, people must learn the way in their own manner, from one point to the next. For example, in the case of the retail store chain, the Third Party believed early in the process that it would probably be advantageous to reduce the emphasis on policing and move toward mutual responsibility and help at that stage. This idea made little sense to the staff. They did not have the personal relationships with the store managers to support it. Nor was the Third Party able to predict the specific arrangement that was decided on. However, it is becoming possible to say more and more about the qualities of the next generation of organizations.*

*III. The "Non-Organization"†*

A common way to deal with a tired old organization is to replace it with a new one. An alternative is illustrated in this case. It consists of setting up an informal, flexible "organization," without permanent formal status, which works with the old organization. This "non-organization" is a changing arrangement of people working together, as described under "Linking" above. It has a core, in this case the DSE and the cochairwomen. It may even make decisions, as here, which are carried out by agreement. It taps into the formal organization as required to take joint action. It benefits from the power to act in the formal organization without being hamstrung by its slowness. It is a way of moving more rapidly than the old organization can, and at the same time helping the old organization to change and grow. The concept has wide utility.

---

* See particularly Robert R. Blake and Jane Srygley Mouton, *Building a Dynamic Corporation Through Grid Organization Development,* Addison-Wesley, Reading, Mass., 1969; and Paul R. Lawrence and Jay W. Lorsch, *Developing Organizations: Diagnosis and Action,* Addison-Wesley, Reading, Mass., 1969.
† We are indebted to Richard Beckhard for this expression.

*IV. Not All Change by Joint Action is Dependent on Confrontation in Small Groups*

Historically, O.D. arose from experiments emphasizing candid communication in small groups. This is still a major focus, and most of the methods in Part Three emphasize this. Small group methods have a lot of power to effect change, as the first two cases attest. However, they are not appropriate to all change strategies. (It was not until the latter part of Phase III that the CTE began to sense a need to give more attention to relationships in the Steering Committee.) The point is that the small group methods should be used in the perspective of an overall change strategy. Even so, they may be helpful for specific problems, such as Case 2.

# Case 4.  Revitalizing a Division of an Engineering Company

Outline of a long-term (over a year) general development effort

"How can you expect to govern a country that has 246 kinds of cheese?"

Charles de Gaulle

STEPS*                                    COMMENTS

## I. Situation                          I

a) A new division manager (D.M.)
was hired by a large corporation to
move a 1000-man division to a
higher level of performance. The
division is a conglomerate of
groups having little contact with
one another and each serving a
broad range of "customers" within
the overall company. Some of the
subunits of the division are very
successful, but many more are lan-
guishing. Many of the subunit
managers are virtual strangers to
one another. Only a few feel that
the previous D.M. had given them
adequate attention, leadership, and
support. The new D.M. undertakes
a long-range organization development program to unify the division, to increase the opportunities
for cross-fertilization and mutual
learning, and to raise his division's
effectiveness.

b) He engages two Third Parties to      b) Many organizations work with a
aid him; one is his personnel man-      consulting team made up of an in-
ager, the other an outside consul-      side and an outside Third Party.
tant. The D.M. and the Third Par-       The insider has the advantage of
ties decide to begin with a Family      intimate knowledge of the organiza-

---

* For an example of a larger and more complex general organizational development
strategy, see S. A. Davis, "An Organic Problem Solving Method of Organizational
Change," *Journal of Applied Behavioral Science*, Vol. 3, No. 1, 1967.

STEPS

COMMENTS

Group Team-building Meeting (pages 117–123) for the senior managers of the division.

tion and its people, plus the ability to move in quickly on opportunities and problems. The outsider has the advantage of knowledge of other organizations, usually more years of experience, and the prestige of an outsider, plus greater liberty to think the unthinkable and to declare the unsayable.

**II.  Family Group Team-building for the D.M.   (3 days)**

**II**

See Family Group Team-building Meeting (pages 117–123).

Here the team-building meeting is intended to consolidate the D.M.'s team and to ensure that the members of the team will undertake ensuing actions jointly.

**III.  An Organization Mirror (See pages 101–105)   (3 hours)**

**III**

Eight persons representing "customer" organizations within the company meet with the D.M. and his top team to give them feedback on how they feel the division functions well and how it functions poorly.

Because the division is made up of semi-autonomous units serving many groups within the company, the Organization Mirror is a particularly useful method for gathering feedback from interested parties.

**IV.  Sensing (See pages 143–146) of Two Sample Groups of First-Level Supervisors and Three Sample Groups of Employees   (5 sessions, $1\frac{1}{2}$ hours each)**

**IV**

STEPS

a) These groups are asked to give their impression of the strengths and weaknesses of the division.

b) The sessions are taped and significant comments on the tapes are later played back to the top team and intermediate levels of supervision.

COMMENTS

Before the sensing begins, the intermediate levels of management are informed of the plan and told that the tapes will be available to them, but will not be used for finger-pointing. Fortunately, there is enough trust in the division to make this statement from top management acceptable. Obviously this would not be true in all organizations.

**II, III, IV**

In studying this organization, these measures provide the top team with four perspectives: their own, the Third Parties', that of their "customers," and that of employees further down in the organization. Not only does the top team gain valuable insight, but it also gains a strong motivation to take constructive action.

**V. Meeting Between the D.M., His Top Team, and the Two Third Parties** (3 hours)

The information collected during the preceding steps is reviewed and discussed, after which the team agrees upon three parallel courses of action: (1) they will set up a manager and supervisory training program; (2) several of the top team

V

STEPS

members will extend O.D. methods downward into their own organizations and others will follow; and (3) they will establish task groups to work high-priority problems, with the membership of each task group drawn from throughout the division.

## VI

a) Manager and supervisor training program.

b) Lower-level team-building, Organization Mirrors, sensing, etc.

c) Problem task groups.

COMMENTS

## VI

a) The group responsible for setting up the manager and supervisory training program is recruited from among the subunits that are to receive the training. The team is guided in its training objectives by the wealth of information that has been collected.

b) Extension of these methods downward is encouraged but with the understanding that organizational units would go ahead only if they really wanted to (O.D. doesn't work very well unless there are people interested). Because each subunit serves a range of "customers," it makes sense for each subunit to conduct an Organization Mirror meeting of its own.

c) The task groups consist of people who have insight and are interested in the problems. Some groups include employees and various levels of supervision; others

STEPS

COMMENTS

include people from the group of eight representing the other divisions in the Organization Mirror (see III).

### VII. Regular Staff Meetings of D.M. and His Top Team

VII

Feedback on progress is made a regular part of the staff meeting agenda.

This is one way of providing the necessary follow-up and critique (see Follow-through, pages 134–136).

### VIII. Recycling Through a Two-Year Period

VIII

a) The D.M. and his top team now hold one team-building session a year (these replace the usual annual meeting). In the last meeting, the next lower level of management was included.

There is no termination point for this kind of change. The objective is to build a capacity for constant change into the culture and activity of the organization.

b) The group providing feedback in the first Organization Mirror has been reconstituted twice to appraise progress.

c) The use of team-building and related methods has gradually permeated downward through the organization.

### IX. Situation as of Today

The D.M. believes that these steps made it possible for him to move into his new assignment more rapidly and with much greater effect.

STEPS

COMMENTS

The members of the top team, who once held one another at bay by means of formal ritual, now join freely in give-and-take. This atmosphere has penetrated to the lower levels. For example, the last top team-building session included the top three levels of management in the same room, and there was free disagreement between the two lower levels of management in the presence of their common boss.

There is now a strong feeling of joint responsibility in the top team. This has resulted in better budget decisions and collaboration on key personnel shifts and the handling of layoffs. Each member of the team takes on a division-wide project for the year, such as career development planning, or the Equal Employment Opportunity program. One joint task group has met 70 percent of the division's cost reduction goals in three months. The team members have learned enough about one another's functions to contribute ideas, and to achieve collaborative action at lower levels. In part as a result of the joint action and the give-and-take, each has been able to improve his management skill materially.

Responsiveness to their "customers" within the company has improved

STEPS

COMMENTS

in such areas as providing realistic cost estimates for services. One useful step was the development of a joint task force to interact with "customers." This task force was made up of people whose regular functions give them good access to "customers." They were given training in the functions of the division, and now serve to link "customers" to available services and collect feedback on the services provided.

Persons outside the division re-mark that managers within the di-vision are working more aggres-sively at improving their functions.

# Summary Observations

This is an example of an effort to move a sizable organization steadily toward a condition of greater health. It is not so dramatic as the specific goal-centered change in Case 1. Progress is slow but improvement is increasingly pervasive. The time frame for clearly discernible change in such an effort is about three years.

The case highlights several points:

○ Things move more rapidly if the impetus to change starts at the top. On the other hand, many successful O.D. efforts have begun just below the top, with the top manager's approval of an "experiment." Success with the experiment then encourages the top manager to involve himself personally.

○ Be sure that use of O.D. methods is voluntary. If top management tries to institute them by directive or pressure, the result is likely to be *pro forma* compliance and failure.

○ In a parochial organization, or one (like most staff groups) that is peripheral to the mainstream of organizational life, the greatest potential impetus to change is most likely to come from the outside, from exposure to the views of other individuals or organizations with which it does business. The more personal and confronting that exposure is, the more likely it is that change will occur, provided that feedback comes in a helpful form and does not simply serve to build up resistance. In this instance the Organization Mirror provided this impetus to change, as did the joint task force described in IX above.

74

# Part Three.  Methods

This part, which is devoted to methods, is divided into four sections. The first section describes meetings to bring about change. In the second section, we offer a series of methods for acquiring knowledge about the current conditions within an organization, even your own. The third section outlines some ways of improving the quality of meetings. In the last section, we present a handful of structural situations that have proven helpful in changing the quality of human relationships. The four maps on the following pages show how the methods are strung together in typical O.D. undertakings.

Along with the description of each method, we have indicated how it might be applied, what its benefits and limitations seem to be, and what operating hints we could pass on. Some of the more complex methods are individually flow-charted.

You will notice that nearly everything that is attempted occurs in the setting of a meeting and that all the methods are framed for as open and lively a confrontation as the participants are willing to enter, not because confrontation is desirable in itself, but because we know of no more direct route to organizational health.

You will detect a number of themes that recur again and again in the following pages:

1. We pay attention to individual as well as group needs.
2. We pool the widest possible range of opinion.
3. We systematically question established ways of doing things.
4. We emphasize feedback and ongoing critique.
5. We clarify interpersonal relationships by deliberately digging out garbage—that is to say, concealed feeling that blocks simple man-to-man understanding.
6. We stress responsibility for sharing management of the enterprise.
7. We encourage exploration of oneself and his connection to others.

For the modern manager and for students of organizational development to whom this book is addressed, we feel prompted to offer opposite admonitions:

1. We hope that you will put these tools to good work in the organizational world in which you live.

2. Once having read it, we hope that you will put this book out of your mind.

The second admonition is another way of saying that we urge you not to proceed mechanically as if this were a book of recipes, but to move with modesty and goodwill toward a kind of organization that is more respectful of human dignity than the world in which you now find yourself and that stimulates human energy and growth.

You will want to approach each meeting with a plan, but you will discover that every group is unpredictable and that you must alter your plan frequently to follow constructive currents that the group sets for itself.

> *"Nothing in progression can rest on its original plan. We may as well think of rocking a grown man in the cradle of an infant."*
>
> *Edmund Burke*

NOTES TO MAP 1

1. Examples of goals:

   To improve your own management performance.

   To improve the management performance of others in your organization.

   To control costs more tightly.

   To raise standards of customer/client service.

   To integrate related functions within an organization.

   To introduce new ideas, methods, technology.

   To change the role of an organization.

   To enter new markets.

   To increase productivity.

2. Example: *Solution:* "We need management development."

   *Problem:* Lower-level managers don't seem to be highly motivated.

   *Comment:* Jumping to the solution frequently leads to incomplete diagnosis and limited alternatives for solving the problem. In this instance, if you can establish conditions (for example, a team-building meeting) in which lower-level managers are free to talk about what's frustrating them, the true nature of the problem, and additional alternatives, may open up. Much of the difficulty may be in what *you* are doing or not doing.

3. Use of O.D. methods may raise eyebrows in other parts of the organization. You're tampering with the established culture.

4. In many organizations, the personnel office is a good place to start looking.

5. Your early change goals will become clearer as you proceed. They will also change as you learn more about what is going on, and as others contribute new ideas and alternatives.

6. A seductive bypass, but you miss the opportunity to develop a better road map.

7. Those with information you need; those with power to affect the outcome of the change attempt; those who can contribute ideas, resources.

8. If you use Map 4, you will need to rethink this.

9. Optional timing: before you start this procedure, or before you start Map 2 or Map 3.

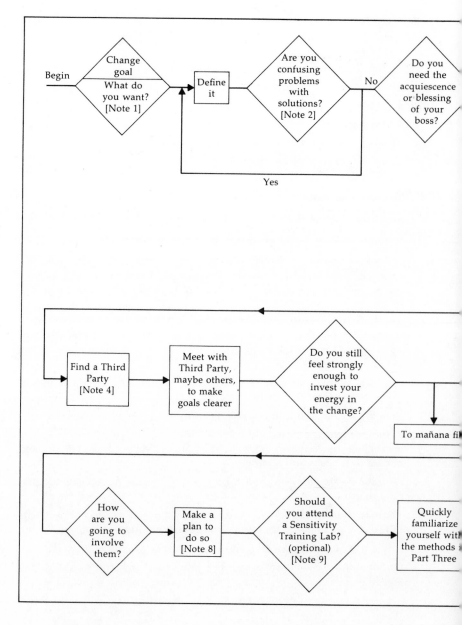

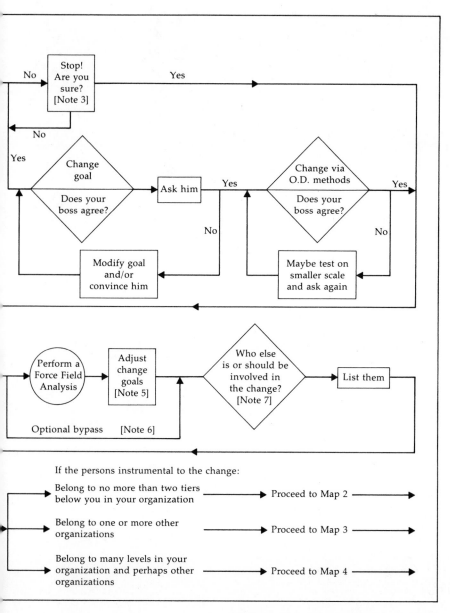

**MAP 1   The Common Road (Typical)**

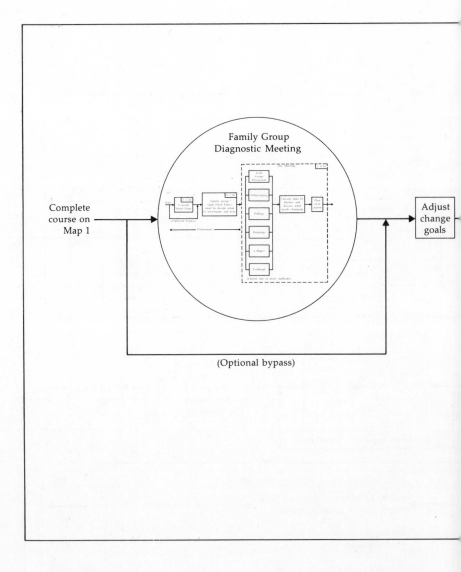

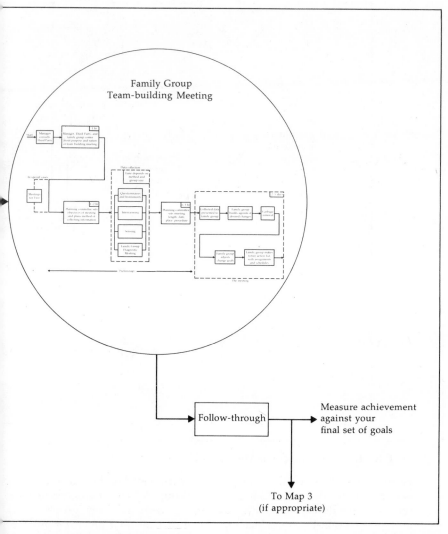

**AP 2   Within a Small Organization**

llow this route after Map 1 if the persons instrumental to the change belong
no more than two organizational tiers below you.

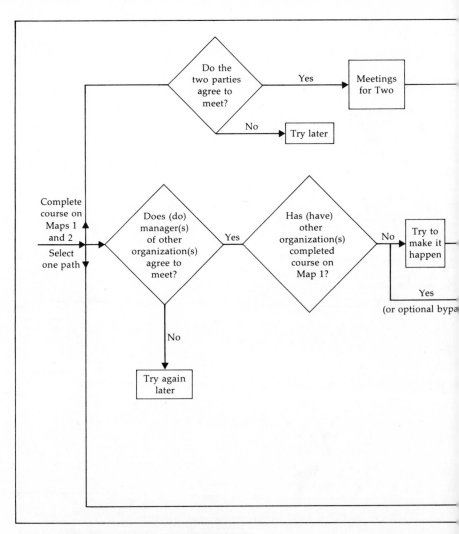

**MAP 3   Interorganizational Methods**

Follow one of these routes if the persons instrumental to the change belong to one or more other organizations. Try Meetings for Two if progress toward change depends on improving relations between two key people. Try Intergroup Team-building Meeting if one or two other organizations are involved, and all of them are willing to consider changing to improve their working relationship. Use Organization Mirror if you want feedback and help from other groups to improve your group's performance and relationships with these groups.

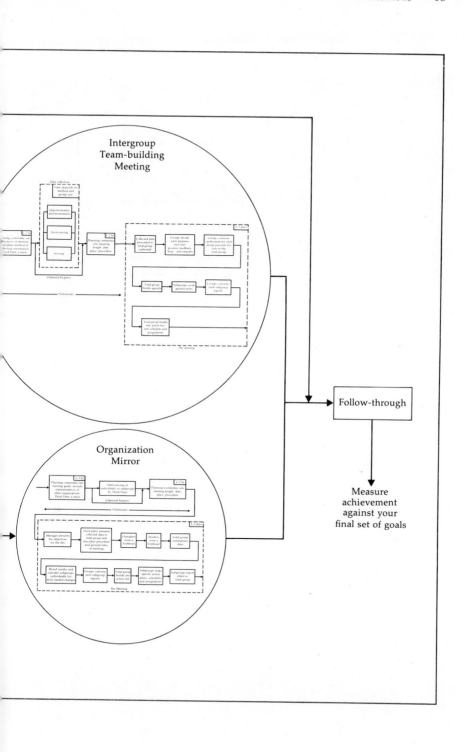

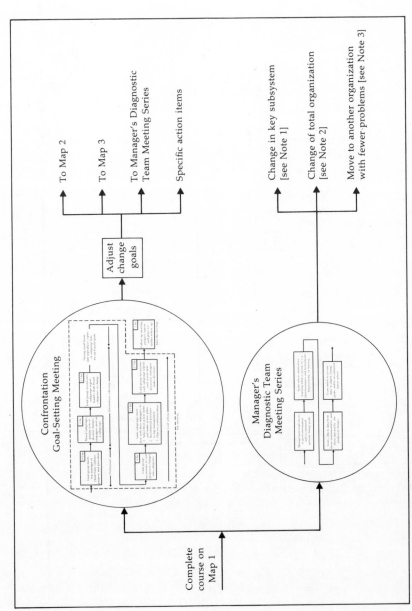

**MAP 4   For Larger Organizations**

Follow one of these routes if the persons instrumental to the change belong to many levels in your organization and perhaps other organizations. If you plan to change the total organization, allow about two or three years.

# NOTES TO MAP 4

1. Example: Case 3.  The Development of a Teacher Education Program

   Other examples: change in the top management structure, in headquarters-field relationships, or in your organization's information system.

   In creating the strategy for change, we can offer no precise road maps. However, there are a number of principles to guide you, and these are presented and exemplified in Part Two.

   a) Provide for working *with* those affected by the change, those with ideas, those with power, and those with interest.  Linking!

   b) Start the linking early.  How change is planned affects how it is carried out.

   c) Don't expect others to be interested in what *you* want unless you're willing to take seriously what *they* want.

   d) Include meetings of a type which will improve the quality of personal relationships (such as team-building meetings).  This is not necessary in every instance.

   e) Remember that change in human organizations can't be planned in detail all the way to the end.  Plan a general strategy, take a step, and then observe where you are before going on, modifying the details of your plan as you proceed.

   f) Provide for feedback through and to the system (see the Organization Mirror, pages 101–105; the Intergroup Team-building Meeting, pages 124–130; and Sensing, pages 143–146).

   g) Will the idea of the "non-organization" (page 64) help?

2. Example: Case 4.  Revitalizing a Division of an Engineering Company

   Other examples: improving communications throughout your organization, or changing management style from Theory X to Theory Y (see Douglas McGregor, *The Human Side of Enterprise*, McGraw-Hill, 1960).

   See the principles in Note 1, and add these:

   a) Don't make a big noise about the changes you hope to make—actions speak louder than words.  But in your personal contacts, make it clear that you are open to change, including changing yourself.

   b) Start as close to the top as possible.

c) Work first with the managers and groups that are most interested in change, so as to fashion early examples of successful change.

d) Be as sure as you can that those using O.D. methods are doing so because they really want to; otherwise it won't work.

e) Make more than "adequate" provision for relearning (see Comment VI, pages 32–33; and Follow-through, pages 134–136).

f) Have your Third Party make available to managers two types of training: "experience-based" exercises which will help prepare them for the world of O.D., and training in O.D. methods (for which this book may serve as one text).

g) Make appropriate use of Sensitivity Training (pages 109–113).

3. Sad, but true.  In some cases it isn't worth the effort.

# *Meetings to Bring About Change*

Since it is in the nature of organization development that most voluntary changes are undertaken with the joint participation of all interested parties, meetings are one of the principal ways through which change occurs.

The 10 types of meetings in this section are presented in a rough sequence corresponding to the order in which you would probably use them. The first five are:

○ The Manager's Diagnostic Team Meeting Series

○ The Confrontation Goal-Setting Meeting

○ The Family Group Diagnostic Meeting

○ The Organization Mirror

○ Force Field Analysis

These meetings focus on diagnosis of the existing situation.

The next four meetings are concerned primarily with altering an existing situation. These are:

○ Sensitivity Training Laboratories

○ Meetings for Two

○ The Family Group Team-building Meeting

○ The Intergroup Team-building Meeting

These are in rough chronological order.  Sensitivity Training may be viewed as basic training for the later meetings.  While Meetings for Two are useful for untangling difficult relationships before a team-building meeting, they may also take place in a later cleanup of problems there wasn't time to settle in the larger meeting.  Family Group Team-building, which applies to organizational units, should take place before intergroup meetings.  It is not efficient to try to bring two groups together if one is preoccupied with unresolved conflicts of its own.  We are not suggesting that an organization needs to continue the four foregoing types of meetings indefinitely.  We see them instead as way stations to a condition of organizational life in which personal needs and relationship problems are dealt with routinely as a normal part of conducting the daily business.

The last type of meeting, the Life/Career Planning Laboratory, is most profitable after you have proceeded a fair way down the organizational development path.

This section concludes with a discussion ("Follow-through") of the morning after and the days beyond successful meetings of the sort described here.

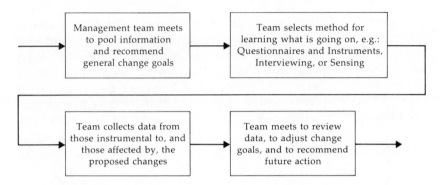

PROCEDURE FOR MANAGER'S DIAGNOSTIC TEAM MEETING SERIES

## 1.  THE MANAGER'S DIAGNOSTIC TEAM MEETING SERIES

*"It requires a very unusual mind to undertake the analysis of the obvious."*

*A. N. Whitehead*

The purpose of the manager's diagnostic team is to make a periodic assessment of the effectiveness of an organization and to entertain the need for and the possibility of change.  The team may meet once or several times.  The team consists of:

○ The top manager or a principal assistant.

○ A Third Party from outside the organization.

○ A staff assistant or assistants with organization-wide responsibility, such as the personnel manager and the administrative or business manager.

The team may be enlarged to include representatives of various levels in the organization as well as individual employees.  The team may also enlist the temporary membership of others, perhaps an operations research consultant or a representative from a related organization.  The reason a manager's diagnostic team is a team rather than an individual is that nearly all organizations are too complex for any one individual to understand. The team meets to pool information on the state of health of the organization and possibly to recommend general change goals and strategies. The team undertakes to gather information by Sensing (pages. 143–146) or Interviewing (pages 140–142), or Questionnaires and Instruments (pages 138–140). The team meets again to consider the collected data and to adjust the general change goals and strategies for action. The manager's diagnostic team may evolve into a steering committee for a long-term O.D. effort.

*Uses*

As an aid to the top manager in examining the health of his organization. (In a large and complex organization, one man can't do it alone.)

As a routine, periodic assessment of the need for change.

*Benefits*

Improves the chances of timely change by bringing together experts in diagnosis with persons intimately acquainted with the organization.

Prompts an organization toward routine self-examination.

*Limitations*

The role of the diagnostic team is limited. It can only stimulate an organization to consider change. If the members are so unwise as to pry secretively or as a team take on executive powers, they are apt to arouse the hostility of managers, planning groups, etc., with the result that fortifications will quickly spring up on what was formerly parkland.

*Operating Hints*

*Role:* No executive powers. No formal fact-finding powers except as these may be jointly shared with the managers involved.

*Frequency of Meetings:* Once or twice a year.

*Team Members:* Persons respected in their organizations who are strongly interested in change.

## 2.   THE CONFRONTATION GOAL-SETTING MEETING*

A large number of persons (usually 40 to 100) from one organization, and its manager, meet for about a day to set goals for change. The meeting has two parts: (1) information collecting and (2) goal setting. A follow-up meeting must be scheduled.

### Information Collecting

Information collecting begins with a description of meeting procedure, followed by a hearty bit of encouragement to frank discussion.

Attendees divide into subgroups of five or six individuals from different parts of the organization. The top managers, less the boss himself, form one subgroup.

The subgroups are given about an hour to arrive at a list of changes that would both please them personally and also benefit the organization. The meeting is open to suggested changes in any area: objectives, organization structure, relationships, management style, procedures, performance, formal and informal policies, etc.

The subgroups prepare their change lists on chart pads (pages 157–159) and present them to the total group, with sufficient commentary to make themselves clear. There is no debate at this time. The changes proposed on the list are sorted into general categories by the meeting leader (or leaders).

### Goal Setting

Each participant receives a copy of all the item lists and the list of the categories. The total group then takes part in classifying the proposed changes into categories.

The group then divides again, but at this time each key manager meets with those attending from his own organization. These subgroups undertake three tasks:

○ To select the three or four items most important to them, and determine what action they will take and when they will start.

○ To select the items to which they believe top management should assign highest priority.

---

\*   This type of meeting was developed by Richard Beckhard.

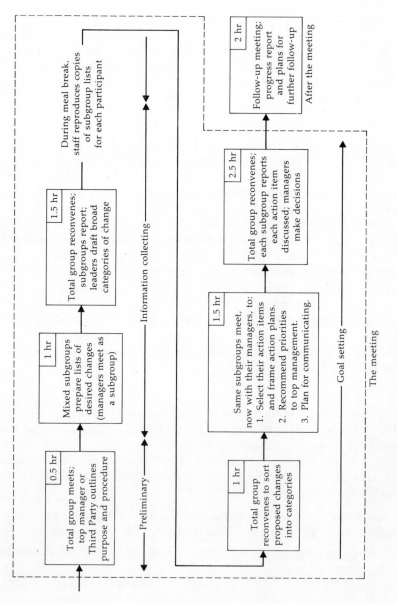

PROCEDURE FOR CONFRONTATION GOAL-SETTING MEETING

○ To plan for communicating the meeting results to others in the organization who are not in attendance.

The total group then reconvenes to hear each subgroup report (with chart pads). There is time for discussion. The top manager makes a decision, even if a preliminary one, with respect to each item referred to him. Plans are laid for the follow-up meeting.

*Follow-up*

The follow-up meeting, normally five to six weeks later, lasts about two hours. Each organization group and the top manager report progress on their change items. Follow-up steps are agreed upon.

*Uses*

For a fast general overhaul of an organization, especially in time of stress.

*Advantages*

Speedy.

The individual becomes more optimistic about working for change because he has more influence over changes and because his own personal needs and goals are legitimized.

Many persons and several levels of management can participate in such a meeting; consequently the method rallies both deep and broad support for change.

It is credible and it makes sense to those involved.

It doesn't require the level of Third Party skills needed for a team-building meeting.

It can bring about major, sometimes even dramatic, improvements.

*Limitations*

The chances are the method won't work well if:

○ there are serious unresolved differences among members of the top management team attending the meeting

○ management is not truly committed to the objectives and mode of the meeting

○ there is insufficient trust among attendees to sustain a reasonable level of candor.

The method isn't likely to bring to light or deal with deep and hard-to-handle issues of management style, performance, relationships, etc. In this sense, it may be viewed as more superficial than many other methods in this chapter, but this fact also reduces dependence on skilled Third Parties. An advantage is that it tends to bring to light only those issues which the group is prepared to confront at this time.

*Operating Hints*

*Key Managers at the Meeting:* Be sure they understand the format and objectives and are willing to go along with the procedure.

*Meeting Introduction:* Present the entire upcoming procedure. Deal with the need for candor. Legitimize personal as well as organizational needs and goals. Allow time for discussion.

*Setting Up the First Subgroups:* You may let them select themselves if you give them two ground rules:

1. Include a representative of each organization present.

2. Don't be in the same subgroup with someone you supervise.

*Charge to the First Subgroup:* Put in writing—handouts, blackboard, or chart pads. Keep the charge broad. If you place limits, you may be shutting off issues of high priority to the group. Until you are willing to listen to them, they will have trouble hearing or getting excited about issues of importance to you. In later meetings, it will be safer to restrict the agenda.

*Meeting Arrangements:* Provide reasonable, uninterrupted privacy for subgroups.

*Third Party:* Not vital to this type of meeting. However, the presence of a Third Party makes people feel safer about raising controversial topics.  The Third Party can also set standards of behavior. He can, for example, check a manager who may belittle earnest complaints.  He may also help modify the day's plan to meet the needs of the particular meeting.

*Follow-through:* Without it, better that you had never begun.  (See Follow-through, pages 134–136).

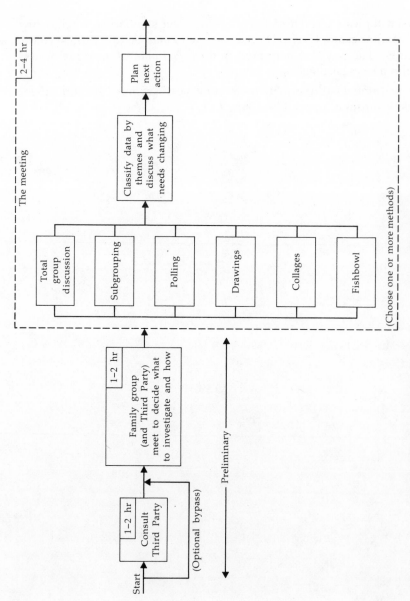

PROCEDURE FOR THE FAMILY GROUP DIAGNOSTIC MEETING

3.  THE FAMILY GROUP DIAGNOSTIC MEETING

A manager and his immediate work group (family group) meet to conduct a general critique of their performance.  The manager can start the action by suggesting categories in which he wants to collect information.

For example:

○ Planning.

○ Achieving goals.

○ What we do best.

○ What we do worst.

○ How we are working together (e.g., management style, how we deal with conflicting points of view, how we do at helping each other and asking for help).

○ Our relations up, down, and sideways.

He may offer these categories at the meeting, or better still, *before* the meeting so that the attendees are able to find out the opinions and sentiments of their own troops.

A variety of methods may be used to collect information, including total group discussion, Subgrouping (pages 162–165), the Fishbowl (pages 165–167), or the various ways of surveying the landscape, especially Polling (pages 146–152), Collages (pages 152–153), and Drawings (pages 153–155).

The information collected is discussed and grouped by themes, and the next action (such as a team-building meeting) is planned.

*Uses*

In advance of a team-building meeting, as a warm-up and to build an agenda.

To help a group decide what change steps, if any, it wants to commit itself to.

*Benefits*

Awakens an adventurous interest in the possibilities of change.

Starts a sharing of the management load.

Prompts more open discussion of problems and relationships.

May effect some changes in individual behavior, though these are apt to be temporary if there is no follow-up and reinforcement.

Flexible; easy to adapt to any group.

Quick.

*Limitations*

It's only a beginning.

It doesn't accommodate a very large group. (Try the Confrontation Goal-Setting Meeting for that, pages 93–97).

It may raise hotter issues than you have time to work through.

*Operating Hints*

*Size of Group:* up to about 30.

*Time:* two to four hours.

*Place:* undisturbed.

People often express a strong preference for working in the total group. This is usually less efficient than subgrouping.

Emphasize listening and understanding. Discourage criticizing and defending.

In holding such a meeting, there is commonly an implied promise of further action. The manager should be prepared to follow through. A recommended sequel to the Family Group Diagnostic Meeting is a team-building meeting (pages 117–123).

*Third Party:* If the group is new to organization development and nothing definite is planned beyond this meeting, a Third Party may spell the difference between going ahead with O.D. and not. A common reason why groups do not proceed further on recognized team problems is that they don't know where to go. The Third Party can offer choices.

4.  THE ORGANIZATION MIRROR

An Organization Mirror is a particular kind of meeting that allows
an organizational unit to collect feedback from a number of key
organizations to which it relates (e.g., customers, suppliers, users of
services within the larger organization). The meeting closes with a
list of specific tasks for improvement of operations, products, or
services.

*Example*

A seven-man central staff group has been laboring to improve its
effectiveness for about a year. Yet the group still experiences friction or indifference from the line groups it is supposed to aid.

To the Organization Mirror, the staff group invites two guests from
each of the line groups. Just before the meeting, the Third Party
interviews all participants, singly or in groups. His purpose is to
prepare the participants for the meeting, learn something about the
size of the problem as they see it, and collect information on the
issues for presentation early in the meeting.

The staff director begins by outlining his objectives for the meeting
and the planned activities of the day. He posts a schedule of activity,
as follows:

*Meeting Schedule*

| | |
|---|---|
| 8:30– 9:00 | Introduction by staff director |
| 9:00– 9:30 | Review of interview data by Third Party |
| 9:30–10:15 | Outsiders fishbowl (pages 165–167) to discuss and interpret the data (insiders listen and take notes) |
| 10:15–11:00 | Insiders fishbowl to discuss what they heard outsiders say and identify issues needing clarification |
| 11:00–12:00 | General discussion to summarize what has happened thus far (ground rule: don't start working problems) |
| 12:00– 1:00 | Break for lunch |

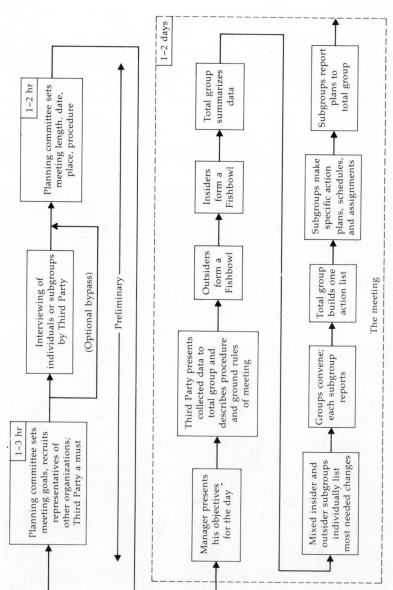

PROCEDURE FOR THE ORGANIZATION MIRROR

| 1:00– 1:30 | Four task subgroups, each comprising both outsiders and insiders, identify the five most important changes needed to improve the effectiveness of the organization |
| 1:30– 2:00 | Reports from subgroups |
| 2:00– 2:30 | Total group synthesizes lists |
| 2:30– 4:30 | The four task subgroups develop a plan and specific action items for change |
| 4:30– 5:00 | Meeting summary—each task group reports plans, action items, persons responsible, and reporting dates. |
| 5:00– 5:30 | Staff director concludes meeting by reviewing day's work and assigning remaining action items |

After the meeting, the Third Party conversed briefly with about half of the participants. The following are some typical reactions to the meeting:

*Outsiders:*

"I think they finally heard what we've been trying to tell them."

"I believe they will get out of their offices now and see what kind of pressure we're under on the line."

"I was encouraged by the way they paid attention to our comments. I don't know if I could have listened to that kind of stuff."

"I have a better sense of all they have to put up with. I'll be a little more responsive in the future."

*Insiders:*

"I was surprised at the number of good things they had to say about us."

"We sure have a lot of work to do!"

*Uses*

When an organization has progressed in team-building, a natural next step is to improve relations with important outside groups.

Particularly useful for staff service groups.

When an organization is being bypassed.

When things seem too good.

When the product isn't being bought.

When a group receives no information (or conflicting information) about its performance.

When a group receives undeserved criticism.

When ability to perform is impaired by other groups.

When interface problems embrace a number of other groups.

### Benefits

Provides feedback simultaneously from a number of sources in a systematic way.

Permits setting of priorities and planning to improve both the organization image and effectiveness.

Often converts critics to helpers.

Converts bellyaching to constructive action.

### Limitations

A complex and demanding procedure that entails some risk of negative outcome.

Typically requires much effort in follow-through.

The process requires careful planning, management, and commitment.

Takes more than a couple of hours.

Needs a skilled Third Party.

### Operating Hints

Allow enough time (1 or 2 days).  Plan the meeting carefully and cleanly divide the time into segments.  As the meeting progresses, permit some latitude for schedule changes, but don't allow planned segments to blur.

The inside and outside groups should be about the same size. The total group should not exceed 20. Select the outsiders carefully. They should be people who are influential and respected in their organizations, who may have some insight into your problems, who are willing to spend the time, who are constructive and articulate but not argumentative. Outsiders should come from groups with whom you do a lot of business.

Encourage both positive and negative feedback. Avoid working troublesome individual relationships. Postpone this for another time.

Record results of all meeting segments on chart pads. Post clearly identified action items for all to see. Don't use this type of meeting only to collect feedback, but do go through the entire cycle of joint planning and execution of changes. It is the latter part that cements relationships.

Commit yourself to a time and method for reporting progress to everyone. Consider inviting the outsiders back at a later time to evaluate progress and give assistance.

## 5.  FORCE FIELD ANALYSIS

Force Field Analysis is a tool for analyzing a situation that you want
to change.  It helps you to alter a condition in an organization with
a minimum of effort and disruption.

The method presupposes that any situation is in a state of equilibrium at any given moment; that is, the forces acting to change the
condition are equally counterpoised by the forces acting to keep it
the same.

The analysis is prepared in the form of a simple diagram:

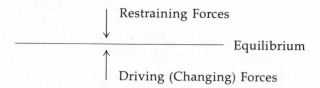

An individual, or preferably a group, begins the analysis of a
given situation in which change is desirable by identifying all the
driving and restraining forces and by assigning arrows to them.

*Example*

A group of foremen are disturbed by the output quality of their parallel production lines.  Rejection rate is 20 percent.  They want to
reduce the rate substantially—say, to 5 percent.  In a brainstorming
session, they name all the pertinent forces and represent them as
follows.  They make the length of the arrows proportioned to the
magnitude of the force.

If you increase those driving forces that threaten or pressure people,
you are likely to increase resistance.  It is better to increase those
driving forces that do not increase resistance or to work on restraining forces, or to consider new driving forces that may be brought into
play.  The foremen concentrate on those forces that are easiest to
change, have the greatest payoff, and, when altered, are least dis-
ruptive.

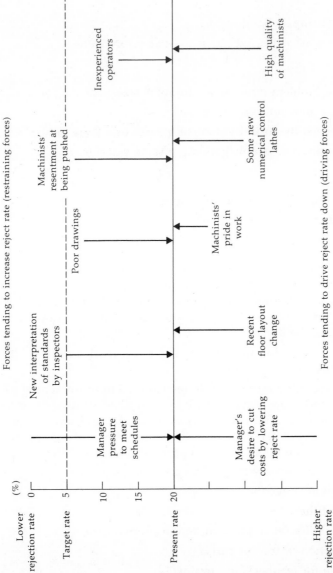

*Uses*

When starting a change effort.

When you are confused about what step to take next.

*Benefits*

Boils the problem down to a "do-able" size.

Opens up new options for action.

Can be used by an individual, or a small or a large group.

Helps a group of people get on the same wavelength.

*Limitations*

Results depend on quality and completeness of analysis.

Sometimes seems overanalytical.

*Operating Hints*

Define the current (equilibrium) condition clearly and determine the desired end result. Press the people to identify as many forces as possible. Stick with it, even though the method may seem a little silly at first. Stick with identification and don't bog down on what can or can't be done.

Include information from as many relevant parties as possible. Use chart pads.

Test to see if the analysis includes motivation of influential parties, policies and procedures, the nature of individual needs and habits, outside forces, administrative practices, financial and material resources, etc. After you have completed the analysis, prepare an implementation plan for the proposed change. Include:

○ The necessary events that must occur.

○ A timetable of events.

○ Names of the relevant people who can help.

○ Responsibility for implementing the subparts.

○ Coordination of the subparts.

○ Provision for feedback and evaluation.

## 6.  SENSITIVITY TRAINING LABORATORIES

*"Men are much more unwilling to have their weaknesses and imperfections known than their crimes."*

Lord Chesterfield

*"God tempers the wind to the shorn lamb."*

Lawrence Sterne

Small groups (usually about 12), together with one or two staff members, work intensively together over an extended period of time (usually three to five days and evenings), learning from their intense ongoing experience with one another in the here-and-now. One learns primarily about the *process* of interaction between individuals in the group, about deeply felt experience and *feelings* as opposed to *intellectual content.*

As a vehicle for personal change and growth, the sensitivity training laboratory has unique characteristics:

○ It is relatively unstructured.  That is, it proceeds without clearly defined goals, rules or procedures, agenda, or member roles.

○ The staff members do not lead in the usual sense. They act primarily as facilitators and climate-setters.

○ The laboratory is a rare opportunity for most men.  Personal and interpersonal data which are produced by here-and-now behavior of members can be examined and learned from.  Also, new modes of behavior can be tested.

○ The climate that a typical group evolves for itself, and which contributes markedly to the learning process, is one of pervasive trust and openness—a human condition of such rarity that the participants are often exhilarated.

*Uses*

As basic training for people who are important to an organization development effort.  Example: a manager who plans a team-building meeting with his group.

To excite the imagination, to open eyes to other and better ways of working together.  In a receptive organization, to generate interest in organization development.

To help someone over a hump in personal growth.  Example: a manager whose effectiveness and advancement are limited by his lack of insight into what he is doing to his colleagues.

*Benefits*

Participants can learn:

About themselves as individuals and how they customarily behave in groups.

About how others respond to them.

About how they in turn look upon and feel about others, and how others influence them.

About how to relate better to others man-to-man and as members of groups.

About the dynamics of groups, including leadership styles, the use of power, subgrouping, hidden agenda, group structure, collaboration and competition, etc.

About the range of choices available to them in responding to others —and that one can indeed choose.

About acquiring skills in effective listening, interviewing, making oneself helpful to others, and allowing others to return the help.

About how to rid oneself of pluralistic ignorance.  (Pluralistic ignorance is the tendency of an individual to assume that a certain joy or agony is his alone, whereas in truth it is known to many.)

About groups that behave as grown-ups: authenticity of behavior (avoidance of maskmanship), the experience of appropriate expression of feeling, use of confrontation, gains from collaboration, and constructive handling of conflict.

For the person who is ready, the laboratory can be a profoundly moving and constructive experience.

Intelligently conducted, these meetings arouse a ferment for change.

### Limitations

Sensitivity training is not for all. Some dislike the intensely personal relationships of the laboratory. Others volunteer so little that they receive little in return.

Occasionally—although quite rarely—someone is psychologically jarred by the experience. Nearly all of these cases seem to involve a prior history of debilitating psychological problems.

The impact of a sensitivity training experience attenuates rapidly. The participant is apt to be highly stimulated by the laboratory and feel that he has immense power to change his life. A few do. For most, the exhilaration fades into memory in a few weeks time. The amount of permanent learning varies widely with the person.

Sensitivity training alone has limited power to change organizations. For a large return on the investment, the learning of sensitivity training needs to be connected to and reinforced by the other types of home organization activity.

There is a good deal of fear and misconception about sensitivity training. If these fears are widespread in your organization, don't use it unless and until the level of acceptance rises. Otherwise you may find yourself fighting the wrong battle (Is sensitivity training good or bad?) instead of the one you want to win: How do we make this organization better?

### Operating Hints

#### Who should attend:

Persons in key positions, especially in organizations which are planning organization development work. (In a team-building session, the more people who have had sensitivity training, the greater the likelihood of a favorable outcome.)

Persons who strongly want to go.

Persons who are ready for personal growth.

*Who should not attend:*

Persons with serious psychological problems.

Problem employees.

Persons under severe stress at the moment.

Persons in psychotherapy, except with their therapist's approval.

Persons who don't want to go.

*Recruitment:* Attendance should be voluntary and the "should not goes" should be screened out. Some ways to do this:

○ Interviews by a qualified person.

○ Opportunity for candidates to talk to someone who has attended.

○ Orientation sessions for a group considering attending.

○ Reading about the subject.

*Quality Control:* There is a wide range of training of this type offered publicly. The quality varies, and the nature of the training varies, some of it seemingly quite bizarre. The fact that it's unusual doesn't mean it's bad, but the style may not be one you seek. Consult with someone who knows the business. The NTL Institute for Applied Behavioral Science, 1201 16th Street N.W., Washington, D.C. 20036, is a good source of information. If you're going to do sensitivity training in-house, you may want to build your own qualified staff of trainers. But it takes years. Don't go with quasi-qualified people except as cotrainers.

*Related Applications*

Most sensitivity training brings together a group of strangers who have never met before and who are to have no continuing relationship. There is a feeling of safety and freedom for the individual in this arrangement. For the sake of organizational payoff, however, it may be worthwhile to sacrifice anonymity.  Here are three possibilities:

1. *Cousin groups.*  These groups consist of people from the same overall organization who have no regular working relationship and, for the most part, don't even know one another.  If you want to do sensitivity training in-house, this is the closest you can get to a stranger group, and it has the benefit of facilitating acquaintanceship across organizational lines.  It introduces a security problem, however.  Can we trust each other not to leak confidential disclosures around the organization where they may be misinterpreted or do someone harm?  Fortunately, the answer is almost always yes, *provided* the agreement is reinforced by group discussion and *provided* that everyone understands that the trainers will not use information from the laboratory, even to help someone, without the permission of the person who volunteered it.

2. *Cluster groups.*  These are like the cousin groups except that the group is made up of several clusters of three or four people who *do* have a regular (nonsupervisory) work connection and who want to improve it.  For example, a cluster might consist of related supervisors from Production, Drafting, and Inspection.  This usually produces an enduring on-the-job improvement.  But it is harder to recruit clusters than cousins.

3. *Family group.** Like the Family Group Team-building Meetings (pages 117–123), this group consists of the manager and the key people who work for him.  The difference is the agenda.  In the team-building meeting, the group makes its tasks its target and deals with relationships and feedback as these become relevant to that primary target.  In the family group sensitivity laboratory, the agenda is limited to relationships in the group as these are revealed in the here-and-now interactions during the meeting.  This brings the intensely personal experience of sensitivity training right into the office.  The payoff on the job is direct and tends to be enduring.  It's only fair to say, however, that the promise of higher payoff must be traded off against a risk of on-the-job repercussions.

---

* Stuart Atkins and Arthur Kuriloff, "T-Group for a Work Team," *Journal of Applied Behavioral Science*, Vol. 2, No. 1, 1966.

7.  MEETINGS FOR TWO

> *"Open rebuke is better than secret love."*
>
> *Proverbs XXVII*

Two persons meet for the specific purpose of improving the way they work together.  They may be supervisor and subordinate, co-workers, husband and wife, or any other duo who share a common goal.  Normally, a Third Party meets with them.  The aims of such a meeting are:

○ To help them lift the "garbage" in the relationship out into the open where it can be disposed of.

○ To specify what each expects of the other.

○ To make clear how each's expectations are not being satisfied.

○ To negotiate changes both in the expectations and the manner of their being met.

○ To increase the mutual helpfulness of the relationship.

There are many ways to conduct such a meeting for two.  The following procedure is highly structured, but it is also nearly foolproof.  (See also the Intergroup Team-building Meeting (pages 124–130).

*Step 1.*  Each person makes up three lists:

○ Positive feedback list: things the person values in the way the two people have worked together.

○ "Bug" list: things he hasn't liked or can't abide.

○ Empathy list: a prediction of what the other has on his lists.

*Step 2.*  Each presents his positive feedback and "bug" lists to the other; then they share their empathy lists.  During this period, the Third Party discourages any talk not directed specifically toward gaining an understanding of the other's point of view.

*Step 3.*  Each then offers any information which may clarify matters.  Again, general discussion is barred.

*Step 4.* The parties now negotiate around changes they want. They consent to planned changes and then decide upon how they will work together to bring them about. The Third Party lists the agreed-upon actions to be taken. He also lists those issues still unresolved. The pair then decides how these will be dealt with, or perhaps agrees that they will be left unresolved for the time being.

*Step 5.* They plan follow-up measures.

*Uses*

For twosomes who are unhappy, angry, frustrated, psychologically divorced, disappointed, defeated, or murderous.

For twosomes seeking a zestful relationship.

High potential payoff for key managers, such as an executive and his assistant, whose relations critically affect the organization they are responsible for.

Useful before a Family Group Team-building Meeting (pages 117–123) if there is a particular trying relationship (e.g., the manager and a key subordinate) which may otherwise block the meeting.

*Benefits*

The procedure is simple, proven, and inexpensive.

Bad feeling between two key people can seriously interfere with the ability of an organization to do its work. A successful treaty between two such individuals can benefit everyone near and far.

*Limitations*

People shy away from it. (Why give up someone to hate?)

The presence of the Third Party may be annoying at first because he is unfamiliar; the formal structure can irritate because it seems contrived.

*Operating Hints*

Not for the routine issues that come along daily. The method is designed for major overhauls.

Both parties must somehow arrive at the meeting in a disposition of good faith, and both must repose confidence in the Third Party. A Third Party is perhaps even more important than in a team-building meeting where the larger groups provide a moderating influence.

Sometimes it is good to enlarge the meeting by including others who know the principals and who can offer valuable insight. This should be done only if both principals agree.

It is important to check the hearing mechanism of the two parties. A way to do this is periodically to ask one person what he thinks the other has just said. (See Hearing, pages 172–174).

The structure and discipline of the meeting can be shaped to the problems and the principals' skill in handling them.

Chart pads (pages 157–159) can be helpful, even for a twosome. Role reversal (see Role Playing, pages 168–170) can be extremely effective in fostering empathy.

Remember that many interpersonal problems are created or relieved simply by new organizational arrangements and job definitions.

Follow-through is important. A follow-up meeting may be scheduled, or the Third Party may later touch base with the parties individually, and bring them together again if necessary.

8.  THE FAMILY GROUP TEAM-BUILDING MEETING

A family group, usually consisting of a manager and those who report to him, meets to explore ways of improving its performance.
The technique applies both to old and new groups.

   The team-building meeting differs from the usual staff meeting
in several ways:

○ It is longer—say, two to five days.

○ It seeks an atmosphere of candid communication about feeling and
   opinion, about the traditional and the informal forces at work in the
   organization (forces such as differences in status, cliques, etc.).

○ The meeting is normally guided by a Third Party.

○ We emphasize the need for joint participation in working through
   the meeting process, from early planning through follow-up, to be
   sure that the group does in fact support whatever is planned and
   done.

   The procedure for a team-building meeting is more or less as
follows:

*Step 1: Setting the Objectives of the Meeting.* While the general objective of the meeting is to improve the effectiveness of the family
group, a specific purpose may be to set goals for the next year. One
purpose of the meeting should always be for the family group to
evaluate its own working process (see Critiquing, pages 160–162).
The task of setting the objectives of the meeting is performed by the
manager, other members of the group that he may select, and the
Third Party (the planning committee).

*Step 2: Collecting Information for the Meeting.* Preferably this is done
before the meeting by Questionnaires or Instruments (pages 138–
140), Sensing (pages 143–146), or Interviewing (pages 140–142). The
Third Party usually leads or performs the task of collecting the data.
Another approach to data collection is the Family Group Diagnostic
Meeting (pages 98–100).

*Step 3: Conducting the Meeting Itself*

The information collected earlier is now presented to the meeting of the family group.

○ The group (or subgroups) now frames an agenda, with topics ranked in order of priority.

○ The group proceeds to heave out the "garbage," i.e., the personal and interpersonal issues that stand in its way. The group rarely follows the agenda it has so laboriously constructed, but this is usually to the good.

○ The group produces a list of action items to be dealt with after the meeting, decides who is responsible for each item, and makes a schedule.

*Step 4: Follow-through* (see Follow-through, pages 134–136). After the meeting, make sure that the agreed-upon actions are taken; also work to maintain the level of candor arrived at in the meeting.

*Uses*

This method can be used for any major meeting of an organization. An occasional meeting of this sort is valuable to any organization whose members want to deal with one another more openly. Frequency depends on the effort the manager wants to put into change.

For a new team, a larger share of the meeting time is allotted to Getting Acquainted (pages 170–172) and planning how the team will function.

*Benefits*

Taps the total knowledge and inventiveness of the group for identifying problems and opportunities.

Builds group commitment to change goals and action steps.

Improves the tone of working relationships.

With new groups, the method accelerates the forming of a tightly knit team.

*Limitations*

Unless the group, and especially the manager, is really willing to move toward open communication, the meeting will be less effective.

*Operating Hints*

*Candor:* The manager must set the standard for candor. The group will test his willingness to face up to their differences with him. Don't raise interpersonal matters unless you have time, help, and commitment to work them through either during the meeting or soon after.

*Responsibility:* The manager must accept lead responsibility for the meeting. The group and the Third Party only share the responsibility.

*Attendance:* You may make attendance compulsory, but you must make it clear that each member is free to take part in the way he chooses.

*Caution:* Don't use a team-building meeting to deal with a hot one-to-one issue, such as the manager's serious complaint about the performance of a member of his group (see Meetings for Two, pages 114–116). Don't conduct a team-building meeting if you plan to fire a member of the group; his dismissal is likely to be attributed to his speaking up (or failing to) at the meeting.

*Length:* Meetings vary in length from one to three days. What is important is that the group feels it has gone "over the top" in meeting the objectives.

> *"Never lick your chopsticks to get at the last grains of rice sticking to them."*
>
> *Tokyo Police pamphlet on etiquette*

For a first team-building meeting, three days is about right. An experienced group may dispose of specific issues in a few hours. Allow enough time to heave out the garbage.

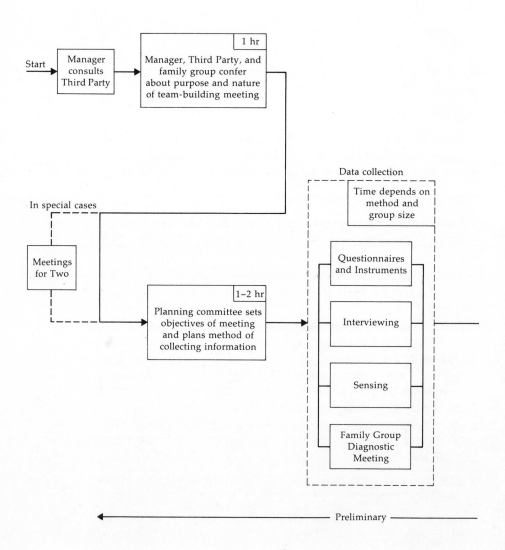

PROCEDURE FOR THE FAMILY

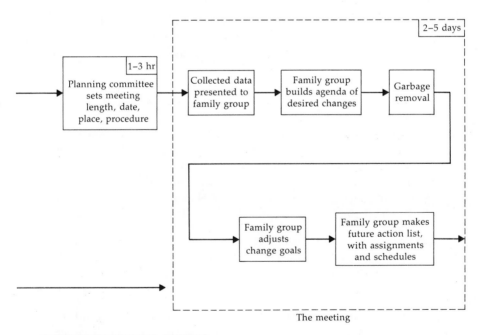

The meeting

GROUP TEAM-BUILDING MEETING

*Meeting Place:* Meet anywhere that the group will not be disturbed. For the first meeting, a comfortable informal setting away from the customary working place is good.

*Group Size:* From 3 to 30. The usual size is 8 to 15. For the larger groups, you'll need to employ Subgrouping (pages 162–165) and the Fishbowl (pages 165–167), as well as allow more time.

*Higher-Management Participation:* Two or more levels of management may attend, but their effect on candor needs to be thought out and discussed ahead of time. One way to involve a higher-level manager is to arrange for him to enter near the end of the meeting, by which time the group will have resolved some of its own issues and prepared an agenda to take up with him.

*Meeting Scope:* Generally too large for the time allowed. Should be restricted to those things the group can do something about. Typically, a lot of time is wasted berating those not present (it's safer).

*Booze:* Cocktail hour should be no more than half an hour.

*Meeting "Balance":* Crucial to a good team-building meeting. Balance refers to:

○ The blend of attention given to relationships versus tasks. Groups usually prefer to work on their tasks and to avoid the interpersonal issues which are getting in their way. Or the opposite can happen; that is, some groups become so intrigued with their relationships that they forget their task. A general rule is to work on the task and to heave out the "garbage" whenever its odor is detected.

○ The "heat" of the discussion. In "cold" discussions, no one has or expresses much feeling. There is a sense of boredom and lifelessness. On the other hand, issues that are too hot to handle can set the group back.

○ The balance of negative and positive feedback. Team-building meetings tend to overemphasize critical information. Positive feedback (pages 174–176) can stimulate the group and pull it together.

*Methods for Conducting the Meeting:* Most of the methods in Part Three have some application to a team-building meeting. Especially, don't forget the use of Chart Pads (pages 157–159) and Critiquing (pages 160–162)!

*Follow-through:* The gains made in a team-building meeting will surely be lost unless serious attention is given to follow-up.

*Not for Intergroup:* Don't use this procedure for interorganizational meetings unless you're planning a merger of some sort.

### Related Applications

The Family Group Team-building Meeting format can be used also for disbanding temporary teams (such as project groups) or for dissolving or substantially reducing "permanent" teams. One or more meetings may be required, depending on the circumstances.
    For the agenda, consider the following topics:

○ Planning the change.

○ Dealing with feelings about the change and the problems posed for members of the group.

○ Planning means for working out new assignments or new employment. (Invite someone from the personnel office.)

○ Use of the Life/Career Planning Laboratory (pages 131–133) for those who are interested.

○ Critiquing the experience of the group for what can be learned.

○ Determining what part of this experience may be helpful to other similar groups and how this information can be transmitted to them.

○ Dealing with the immediate problems of the remaining group.

○ Planning its future.

## 9.  THE INTERGROUP TEAM-BUILDING MEETING

*"Peace (noun)—In international affairs, a period of cheating between two periods of fighting."*

*Ambrose Bierce*

Two groups meet to improve their working relationships.  The purpose of the meeting is to reach a state of mutual understanding that fosters cooperation and cuts down on isolation, competition, and strife.  The process involves:

○ A deliberate effort to surface concealed resentment and mistrust (garbage).

○ An attempt to distinguish fact from fancy.

A search for ways in which the two groups can serve each other better in achieving common goals.

○ A determination to be explicitly helpful.

A typical procedure for the meeting follows.  As in the case of the Family Group Team-building Meeting (pages 117–123), the procedure is public in the sense that all cards are laid on the table, and all participants are informed of what is in the offing and are encouraged to speak their piece at any stage.

*Step 1: Setting the Objectives of the Meeting.*  The scope and objectives of the meeting are set by a planning committee.  The committee consists, at a minimum, of the managers of the respective groups and a Third Party.  The committee meets to:

○ Disclose its impressions of current relationships between the two groups.

○ Decide what additional information is needed before the groups come together, and how it will be collected.

○ Outline the procedure to be followed during the meeting and the follow-up work.

Decide who should attend, and the time, length, and place of the meeting.

*Step 2: Collecting Information for the Meeting* (Optional).   Refer to Step 2, page 117.

*Step 3: Conducting the Meeting Itself.* The objectives and procedure of the meeting are made clear.  The information collected in Step 2 (optional) is now presented to the whole meeting on chart pads.
   Each group meets separately to prepare three lists:

○ Positive feedback list: things the group values in the way it has worked with the other group.

○ "Bug" list: things the group dislikes.

○ Empathy list: a prediction of what the other group has on its lists.

   The groups now come together.  A spokesman for each presents his group's lists.  During this period, the Third Party discourages any discussion not directed specifically to clarification of the other group's point of view.  Then the total group prepares a working agenda and sets priorities.
   Subgroups are formed to work each item of the agenda and to report back to the total group. It is important that both organizations be represented on each subgroup.  One or more of the subgroups may be asked to Fishbowl (pages 165–167) in the presence of the total group, after which the audience critiques the Fishbowl members for their skill and willingness in helping one another.
   The subgroups report back to the total group, which then formulates a list of action items that it commits itself to perform.  The action items are assigned and scheduled.

   The group adjourns for refreshments.

   *"An empty stomach is hostile to every form of joviality."*
                                                        *Norman Douglas*

*Step 4: Follow-up* (See Follow-through, pages 134–136).  After the meeting, follow-up activity must ensure that the agreed-upon action

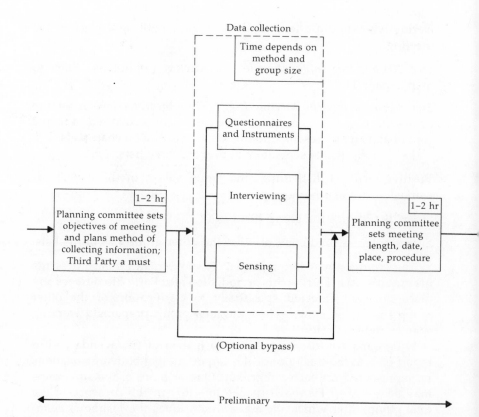

PROCEDURE FOR THE INTERGROUP

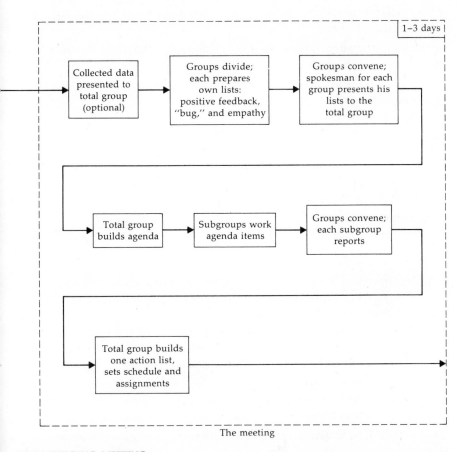

The meeting

TEAM-BUILDING MEETING

items have been performed and that the level of open communication arrived at in the meeting is maintained.

*Uses*

A specific remedy for parochialism, the medicine is extremely beneficial whenever working relations with another organization seem simply too hard and you wish to ease the pain by performing the other group's functions within your own organization.  Relieves finger-pointing fever.

When properly administered and with adequate after-care, the treatment is free of injurious side effects.

Use may be safely prescribed for the classic maladies that affect relations between:

○ Staff and line.

○ Headquarters and field.

○ Supplier and customer.

○ Engineering and manufacturing.

○ Specialist group A and specialist group B.

○ Your tribe and mine.

*Benefits*

Your organization was probably designed to function in collaboration with other groups.  The intergroup meeting is a way to restore interdependent activity to design specifications.

The method is cheaper than squirming around or trying to blast through all the roadblocks that seem to spring up spontaneously in the communication channels between working groups.

The method helps to disburden an overloaded chain of command. In a complex modern organization, the top manager hasn't time to settle all the feuds and squabbles that go on underneath him.

As a tonic, it stimulates health and vigor in intergroup working relations.

*Limitations*

While the medicine is specific, it is not magical. Intergroup relations can be tough and may require continuing attention to detail. The intergroup meeting, however, is an excellent way to set the stage for further cooperation. But watch out for backsliding.

Groups often resist the treatment. It's hard for many groups to comprehend just how poor their relations are. ("Organizations and people are just naturally this way.")

There's also a fear that the cure may be worse than the disease. ("We're so used to war, peace could kill us.")

*Operating Hints*

*Candor:* The managers must set the standard for candor. They will be tested by the other participants.

*Responsibility:* The managers must accept lead responsibility for the meeting. They must first understand what they're getting into.

*Attendance:* Invite the people who can solve the problem you agree to solve.

*Caution:* Don't go into an intergroup meeting if you haven't solved serious internal problems; these will contaminate the process of working with another group. Perhaps a Family Group Team-building Meeting (see pages 117–123) is in order first.

*Length:* One-half day to two days, more if necessary. The group members must feel they have gone "over the top" in meeting the meeting's objectives.

*Meeting Place:* Anywhere the groups will not be disturbed.

*Group Size:* From 4 to about 30.

*Meeting Scope:* Should be restricted to those things the attendees can do something about. Either have the right people there or limit the scope and the expectations.

*Discipline:* Follow the planned procedures and schedule. Change only upon careful deliberation and for good reason. Confront anyone who slips away from the spirit and/or agreed-upon procedures.

*Cultural Differences:* In meetings between groups from different kinds of organizations, such as a supplier and customer, look for (and bring out into the open) basic differences in work cultures and roles which may create "noise" in their communications. For example, in some organizations people are freer to speak out and act independently than in others. Allow more time for meetings between groups from different types of organizations.

*Emphasis:* During the meeting, search for ways in which the groups can help each other. Subgrouping with mixed membership is one way of doing this. Highlighting collaborative ideas or specific offers of help is another.

*Follow-through* (See pages 134–136): After the meeting, follow-through is the key to success. Here are some specific suggestions for follow-up intergroup meetings:

○ Schedule a shorter, follow-up meeting four to six weeks after the first meeting.

○ Keep the subgroups that were established at the meeting functioning until their job is really done and the results put into practice. Continue to use *ad hoc* mixed-membership subgroups as needed.

○ Invite a representative of the other group to meetings in which there is a joint interest.

## Related Applications

This format can be used for the first phase of a merger meeting. In this case, the lists prepared by the groups should cover:

What they like about the merger.

What they are concerned about.

Their prediction of the other group's lists.

The second phase should be like the Family Group Team-building Meeting (pages 117–123), with the total group working in concert around its new joint goals and organization.

At the beginning of the meeting, the manager needs to be specific as to which decisions are firm, and which decisions are open to deliberation by the group.

10.  LIFE/CAREER PLANNING LABORATORY*

> *"Man has to live with the body and soul which have fallen to him
> by chance. And the first thing he has to do is to decide what he
> is going to do."*
>
>                                            *José Ortega y Gasset*

Working in subgroups of four, participants are given the following
instructions:

"Think about your past life, your present, and your future. Then
prepare a Collage (pages 152–153) using any pictures, words, or
drawings that seem significantly related to your past, present, or
future. Don't worry about whether you can explain that relationship. Go by feeling. After the collage is finished, post it on the wall."

After the collages are posted, further instructions are given:

"Now imagine that you have died 10 years from now. Write a letter
from one of your best friends to another good friend, telling about
you and your life. What do you *want* him to be able to say about
you? Next, imagine you have been killed in an auto accident next
week. Now write a similar letter. What would he be likely to say
about you?"

Each participant then presents his collage to the three other members
of his group and reads them the two letters he has written.

   With this as a background, each participant prepares a "Life Inventory" by answering these questions:

○ What do I do well?

○ What do I dislike doing that I must do in my present circumstances?

○ What do I want (need) to do better?

○ What dreams do I have, i.e., wishes that I have not turned into plans?

---

\* We are indebted to Dr. Herbert A. Shepard of the Yale Medical School
for his contributions to this laboratory method.

Each attendee now prepares a "Career Inventory" (as a subset of "Life Inventory"), which answers the following questions:

○ What kinds of work experiences give the greatest satisfaction?

○ Which of my skills and talents are most highly valued by the organization?

○ What are my flat sides in the work environment in terms of interpersonal competence, technical competence, managerial competence, etc.?

○ What do I dislike in my present situation?

○ What rewards mean the most to me—status, money, power, recognition, achievement, security, sense of growth, sense of challenge, risk-taking, winning, close team relations, doing my own thing, etc.?

○ What new career areas would I like to explore?

○ What new skills do I want to develop?

○ These "Career Inventories" are also discussed with the other members of the group.

   Finally, each participant brings this earlier work into focus by writing down goals, steps to be taken to reach them, and target dates.


*Uses*

Particularly useful at critical career points.  For example:

○ You are contemplating a new job opportunity.

○ You are a fairly senior technical man and you expect to be offered, or wonder if you should apply for, a managerial opening.

○ Like most men in their 40's you begin to raise fundamental questions about what you want to do with the rest of your life.

As part of a Sensitivity Training Laboratory, or even a team-building meeting, or as a special meeting just for this purpose, or maybe a one-man task, or working with someone who knows you well, such as your supervisor or your wife.

*Benefits*

Helps get you out of a rut and gives you more control over your life.

Honest discussion helps you to separate daydreams from real possibilities, what you would like from what you want most.

You may thus stop blaming your fate on the organization or the pitiless stars and accept responsibility for your own decisions.

It makes sense to plan your career in the context of your whole life.

*Limitations*

If you want to hold people in jobs to which they are not really committed, you may not like the results. Many will come out with an urge to try something new.

Be prepared for the ferment that may follow Life/Career Planning.

Watch your motives in inviting someone to a Life/Career Planning Laboratory. Are you seeking an easy way to get rid of or mold people?

*Operating Hints*

Be careful that the selection process for attendees recruits only those you really want to spend the time and money on, not only for the laboratory, but also helping them with their new plans.

Avoid amateur psychoanalyzing. It is not helpful.

Follow-up is a necessary part of the procedure. Supervisors of attendees should be aware of their obligation to assist. Normally, wives are involved. It is a good idea for participants to take home the papers they prepare in the process. Living for a while with one's collage frequently stimulates new insights.

Allow one or two days for a meeting concerned solely with Life/Career Planning.

Skilled Third Parties can help to make the experience richer. While they are not essential, they are a good investment.

## 11.  FOLLOW-THROUGH

The trouble with meetings that are intended to bring about change is that they inspire optimistic expectations—and then . . . maybe nothing happens.

It's not through bad intentions, or carelessness, or accident that the meeting itself may become a trap.  Let's look at what follows a successful team-building meeting.

A few may be disappointed.  They came with high hopes; perhaps they relied on the Third Party or the manager or someone else to wave a magic wand.  But there are many problems that require continuous attention over years—such as reaching the point where everyone shoulders his responsibility for openly confronting the things that bother him, or where people can be counted on not to lash out or withdraw in the face of negative feedback, or where they know how to fight fair and enjoy it.

But most likely the attendees have become turned on.  They feel closer to one another.  They have dealt with some things that they were never able to deal with before.  They feel freer and more able to move out toward group and personal goals.  And they have made resolutions about what they're going to do to improve things, recorded as action items.  And so on.  Yet as weeks of routine life at the office pass by:

○ The action items start slipping.

○ We start sliding back into old ways of avoiding issues.

○ We start to wonder if someone, especially the boss, is mad at us for something we said at the meeting.

○ We lapse into doubt that a brave new world will ever come.

The lesson is obvious.  One-shot fixes don't fix.  Good results depend on long-term action.

Here is a buffet of suggestions for follow-up:

Make your next staff meeting a little longer.  Invite your Third Party. Use the time to report on the status of action items and to conduct a postmortem of the past meeting:

○ How do you feel about the meeting now?

○ Are we slipping?  How?

○ Did anything come up at the meeting that you now feel uncomfortable about?

○ Did we make any decisions we should reevaluate?

○ Is there anything that didn't come up then that we should take up now?

○ Meetings for Two (pages 114–116).

○ Build a Critique (pages 160–162) into your meetings.


Include the Third Party role in your meetings.  You can invite an experienced Third Party or you can assign the role to someone in your group, perhaps on a rotating basis.  His job is to monitor the effectiveness of the meeting.  For example, he may call attention to evidences of boredom, frustration, irritation, uneven participation, getting off the track, or lack of clarity.

Set up a foolproof system for monitoring and reporting on action items.  Failure to do so is demotivating and may be viewed as a breach of faith.  You may give the monitoring job to your secretary, a staff member, or your Third Party.  Just be sure to give the job to someone who's tenacious.

If the meeting was an intergroup type of meeting (Organization Mirror, pages 101–105, or the Intergroup Team-building Meeting, pages 124–130), you may want to invite representatives from the other groups to some of your meetings.

Consider fanning out or down in the overall organization with similar meetings.  For example, if you have just had a team-building meeting with your own group, and many of the problems identified at the meeting center around relations with another organization, your next major step may be to arrange an Intergroup Team-building Meeting with that organization.

You'll probably be ready for another team-building meeting yourself in six months or a year.

Maintain a file of the history of your efforts to change and improve your organization. Keep in it a record of issues, insights, and action items from each meeting you have. It will give you a sense of perspective and direction, and jog you if you keep making the same mistakes or repeatedly fail to deal with the same set of tough problems.

# Methods for Finding Out What is Going On

This section contains seven basic methods for collecting information. They include:

○ Questionnaires and Instruments

○ Interviewing

○ Sensing

○ Polling

○ Collages

○ Drawings

○ Physical Representation of Organizations

The methods are ranked in order of degree of confrontation. Thus Questionnaires are generally relatively impersonal because the source of the information is not publicly revealed, while Physical Representations (in which, for example, participants literally position themselves according to degree of influence) are highly confronting.

As a rule of thumb, the more confronting the method, the richer the response and the stronger the impulse to change. But groups vary considerably in their readiness to work with intimate methods.

Another important method for collecting information is Subgrouping. However, Subgrouping has more general uses and consequently is described in the section on Methods for Better Meetings (pages 157–167).

### 1.  QUESTIONNAIRES AND INSTRUMENTS

*Questionnaires* are an old standby for detecting sentiment.  We send out questionnaires to customers, production workers, the professional staff, constituents, television and movie viewers, lower levels of management, people who sojourn at motels and ride in planes. An indication that our restless students have begun to achieve their goals will be their receiving a set of questionnaires (instead of tests) from the managers of education.

Unfortunately, traditional questionnaires have often been disappointing as a means of bringing about significant change within organizations.  They do not create the kind of personal involvement and dialogue that is so valuable in changing hearts and minds.  The information garnered by questionnaires tends to be canned, anonymous, ambiguous, and detached—i.e., cool data rather than hot. The replies may be interesting but they lack punch.  It is too easy to hold them at arm's length, put off until another day, take token action.  And the questionnaire asks the person only what *we* want to know, not what he thinks we should know.  You might say a filled-out questionnaire amounts to about half a conversation.  The employee opinion questionnaire is regarded by many as a device that some managements use to avoid coming to grips with deep sentiment.

Nevertheless, to our mind the questionnaire can be useful when it is developed jointly by the manager and representatives of the population he wishes to canvass.

The *instrument* as used in organizational development is similar to the questionnaire, with the important addition that it is constructed around a theory of management in such a manner as to help the user understand the theory and rate himself or his organization in terms of that theory.  Thus in "Grid Organization Development" (refer to the Bibliography at the back of the book), the manager answers questions which help him place himself in the grid model of management styles.  Others in the group rate him too.  In this manner, instruments are a means by which a group can collect information from itself about itself.  This information then provides the starting point for feedback and confrontation within the group.

*Uses*

As a primary vehicle for learning in one complete system of organization development (Grid Organization Development).

To collect information as part of a specific, planned strategy of change, preferably jointly managed.

Instruments may be used by a group to collect information quickly about itself, as part of a diagnostic or team-building meeting. In this use, the instrument is the same as Polling (pages 146–152) except that the instrument is predesigned and may incorporate criteria for evaluation.

*Benefits*

Questionnaires and instruments are economical for gathering information from a large population.

They lend themselves readily to legitimate statistical use.

Instruments are valuable for self-confrontation, for learning, and as stepping stones to interpersonal confrontations.

You can afford to spend time and money on quality.

There is wide acceptance of these methods.

They reduce reliance on expert Third Parties.

Anonymity may bring to light previously undisclosed strong sentiment.

*Limitations*

Questionnaires and instruments produce findings which seem "canned," a quality which is mitigated if they are used, as in Grid Organization Development, as a stepping stone to confrontation. The hazard is that the parties involved may merely imitate the motions of engaging with one another—shadowbox, so to speak.

One becomes too readily dependent on the questionnaire, pressing upon it (and thrusting away from oneself) a load it can't carry: real human communication.

*Operating Hints*

Unless the objective is purely personal learning, be sure the questionnaire or instrument leads to real engagement between people. Are those involved really hearing each other well enough—both heart-to-heart and head-to-head—so that their communication will have consequences in constructive action?

## 2.  INTERVIEWING

Before a team-building or similar meeting, it is common practice to interview the participants.  The interviewer is generally a Third Party.  The purpose of the interview is to explore ways in which the group can be more effective.  The interviews uncover both positive and negative opinions and sentiments about a wide range of subjects—for example, clarity of individual and group goals, impact of the manager's style, and personal concerns that have never been aired.

The questions should help the interviewee to express whatever is on his mind about life in the organization.  Examples of general opening questions:

"How are things going around here?"

"What changes would you like to see?"

"How do you think this organization could be more effective?  What do you feel it does best?  Does poorly?"

The interviewer may also ask about management:

"How would you describe the management style of Mr. X?  How do you think he could be more effective?"

Questions may also be asked about relationships within the organization:

"Whom do you like to work with most?  Least?"

"Who is most influential in your organization?"

"Are you kept informed of what goes on?"

And about relationships with other organizations:

"When there are problems with other organizations, what can you do about them?"

"Can you give examples of unresolved issues with other organizations?"

"Do you think you could give them advice that would help them do a better job?"

Information from the interviews is fed back to the total group, usually at the beginning of the meeting.

*Uses*

Interviewing is a way to get private views and feelings out on the table. The information collected often furnishes the principal basis for the meeting agenda.

*Benefits*

The interview is an excellent way to probe for the problems and opportunities of the organization. Interviewing has the virtue of facilitating private expression. A sensitive interviewer can also invite ideas and emotions that the subject has not previously formulated in any conscious way. Interviewing also furnishes an occasion to develop trust between the Third Party and members of the organization; such trust is valuable in later work.

*Limitations*

A good interview often takes one to two hours. For a large organization, interviewing can therefore consume a lot of time.

Skillful interviewing runs the risk of turning up more information of a personal and perhaps threatening nature than the group is ready to deal with. When confronted with the interview findings, the group may close up, reject the information, and attack the interviewers.

If the interviewer is clumsy, or if his neutrality is suspect, interviewing may worsen matters. Under these circumstances, it is better to gather information by open group process. (See methods 3–7 in this section.)

*Operating Hints*

There should be an understanding between the interviewer, the manager, and members of the team as to how the information will be used, especially with respect to protecting the privacy of sources. Normally, interviewees are promised that the information will be presented anonymously. The interviewer must keep his promise.

The information can be presented verbatim or thematically. The former has greater impact but does not protect privacy as well, and some data may be too hot for the group to handle. Thematically presented material has the opposite virtues: it's cooler, protects privacy better, has a softer impact. It is usually easily summarized, and hence easier to grasp.

One variation in reporting is to present themes and to back them up with supporting verbatim quotes.

If the findings are highly critical of the manager or another member of the group, it is advisable for the interviewer to disclose enough of the information to the manager in advance of the group meeting so that he will not find himself under surprise attack.

Interviews may be carried out on an individual or subgroup basis, the latter having the obvious advantage of saving time. Interviewing of subgroups does not confer the same advantages of privacy and sensitivity, but the information disclosed tends to be of a character that the group is ready and willing to deal with. Moreover, the person who volunteers data in a subgroup interview normally feels committed to confirm it in a larger meeting.

A way to disseminate the interview findings is to type and distribute copies to all members of the group. Summary statements and corroborative information can then be posted on chart pads (see pages 157–159).

## 3.  SENSING

Sensing is an organized method by which a manager can inform himself of the issues, concerns, needs, and resources of persons in his organization with whom he has limited personal contact.  It takes the form of an unstructured group interview and is usually tape-recorded.  The recording may be then used to educate others.

*Example*

The general manager of a 2000-man organization wants to make his annual report to employees highly pertinent to their interests.  To discover what subjects most concern them, he asks his personnel manager to schedule a series of meetings with a sampling of employees.

The personnel manager schedules four meetings, each two hours in length and each with a different group of 12 employees.  To aid the general manager get a "feel" for people in all parts of the organization, the personnel manager selects the attendees as follows:

*Group I*—Nonsupervisory, shop and service, and technical and office employees.

*Group II*—Professional employees and staff specialists.

*Group III*—Supervisors.

*Group IV*—A diagonal cross section (i.e., one person from each organizational level; no one of the persons selected reports to any other).

Before scheduling the meetings, the personnel manager contacts the supervisor of each prospective participant.  He explains the purpose of the meeting and the intention that no direct actions will ensue which might affect the supervisor or people who report to him.

Each meeting begins with a statement from the personnel manager.  He says that the general manager will arrive in half an hour.  He explains the general manager's purpose for the meeting and his hope that the conversation will be open and informal.  The personnel manager suggests: "Suppose you board an airplane to Europe and you happen to find yourself sitting next to the general manager. What would you say to him?" He also tells the group that he would like to tape-record the meeting primarily to ease the burden of note-taking. The general manager may also later use the tape to refresh his memory or to present illustrative excerpts to the division's top staff. If any member of the group prefers, he will promptly turn off the tape now or at any time during the conversation.

During the meeting, the general manager spends most of his time listening, sometimes asking questions to ensure that he understands what is being said. He also expresses his own thoughts and intentions regarding the various topics introduced.

*Another Example*

A manager has been hearing from outsiders that recently hired engineers in his organization are dissatisfied. To better understand the nature of their complaints, he asks the personnel manager to arrange sensing sessions with several groups of engineers and a group of engineering supervisors.

*Uses*

To collect information as part of a general diagnosis of the organization. (See the Manager's Diagnostic Team, pages 91–92).

To learn the desires and agonies of a group that seems to be dissatisfied.

To learn how organization objectives are understood by diverse people within an organization.

To test a proposed course of action for its impact on various groups of people.

*Benefits*

The interaction of the group often produces rich information and ideas.

More economical than individual interviews.

May provide a quick glimpse of what's going on.

Allows for communication of impressions and feelings as well as opinions and ideas.

Provides a check on conventional and more formal communication channels.

Admits the rumble of humanity into the ivory tower.

Tapes from sensing sessions communicate more vividly to later listeners than secondhand transmission, written reports, or questionnaires.

## Limitations

Won't work well unless the relations at various levels in the organization are basically trusting.

Is not as statistically rigorous or as economical as a questionnaire.

May be suspected as "snooping."

Success of the meeting is highly dependent on the manager's ability to listen effectively and on his willingness to engage with the members of the group in a personal way.

The meeting may fail to get at the attendees' real concerns because for one reason or other they are not willing to reveal them. The manager may thus be spoofed by a fish they toss at his feet.

## Operating Hints

Make sure that all intermediate supervisors understand the objectives and possible outcomes of the meeting so that they will not feel "spied upon." Be clear and explicit about the objectives of the meeting and what is to become of the information.

Note-taking may interfere with easy, informal discussion and the tape recorder is less likely to. But tape-record the session only if the group is willing. Be explicit about how the tape will be used and make a commitment to control its use.

Don't try to use sensing as a substitute for maintaining effective communication channels throughout the organization, or to "get the boss's message across," or to reprimand or judge.

Allow about two hours (enough time for a comfortable discussion).

Provide some warm-up time with a Third Party, especially for people who have never seen the big boss.

Convene the session in a comfortable setting and one which is not strange to the group (don't meet in the boss's office).

Establish a single and limited objective for a given sensing session. Don't try to cover too much at once. Start the meeting in an open-ended way. This will permit individuals to express their viewpoints (e.g., "How does it feel to work around here?" or "I'm interested in how things are going," rather than, "Do you like the company benefits plan?").

If the manager doing the sensing is a poor listener, include a Third Party who, by prearrangement with him, can intervene if he seems to be blocking the group's efforts to express itself.

Don't do a lot of sensing unless the groups sensed can see positive results coming from it. Overuse of sensing can be as bad as overuse of questionnaires. Sensing may be conducted by other persons than a key manager; for example, by a Third Party or someone from the personnel department.

## 4.  POLLING

Sometimes a group becomes uneasy with itself. The members may feel anxious, bored, or in some way out of tune with one another. Such conduct is a common symptom of a buried issue. The way out is to move the discussion to the unspoken agenda item. Polling is a way to reveal it. Or, in a more positive way, a group may wish to evaluate its current state as a prelude to action.

One approach is to poll the group on a question that calls attention to its present condition. The Third Party might float a tentative question and, with the help of the group, modify the question so that it becomes one that the group wants to deal with. The participants must also decide upon the procedure for conducting the poll.

### Example

The group has been planning goals for improvement. At this time, the discussion is agreeable but lethargic. The Third Party suggests polling the group members on their optimism about whether they can agree upon and later achieve a goal involving significant change. The group consents. He suggests a procedure. At the blackboard he draws a scale of optimism:

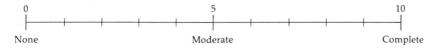

He asks each member to assign a number to his degree of optimism. The Third Party will mark each response on the scale. The group agrees.

The responses cluster around $2\frac{1}{2}$. Now the group members begin to comment on their pessimism, on their history of past failures at meeting their goals. They begin to analyze weaknesses in their methods of planning and execution of change. More than one member acknowledges a feeling of guilt because he has not been able to subscribe to the manager's wishes and has done instead what he felt he had to do.

The truth begins to sink in. As a group, they have a way to travel before they can plan realistic goals to which they will feel strongly committed.

### Another Example

One person remarks that participation in the meeting has been uneven. Some have said little or nothing. Others have made important comments to which there was no response; perhaps they have not been heard. One or two have dominated the conversation.

The group determines to poll itself on this concern. The members will score one another (from 1 to 5) on two questions:

○ Amount of participation?

○ Quality of participation?

Each member writes down his rating of himself and the others on the two questions. The results are presented to the group on grids, one grid for each question:

SUBJECT: AMOUNT OF PARTICIPATION

*Raters*

| | John | Joe | Ted | Sam | Ray | Fred |
|---|---|---|---|---|---|---|
| John | ② | 1 | 1 | 1 | 2 | 1 |
| Joe | 5 | ⑤ | 5 | 5 | 5 | 5 |
| Ted | 4 | 5 | ③ | 4 | 4 | 5 |
| Sam | 2 | 1 | 2 | ① | 2 | 2 |
| Ray | 1 | 2 | 1 | 1 | ③ | 1 |
| Fred | 1 | 1 | 1 | 1 | 1 | ② |

*Subjects* (row label, vertical)

Circled numbers are self-ratings

Following the poll, the group members agree on the need to police themselves better. They also decide to rotate responsibility for calling attention to weaknesses in future meetings.

### Another Example

One member wonders aloud about how effective the group is as a team. The Third Party suggests that the members first decide upon the attributes of an effective team (in their situation) and then rate themselves on each attribute.  The group now *develops its own* questionnaire, which is posted.  Each member now marks his ratings:

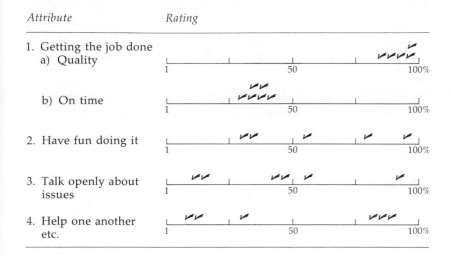

| Attribute | Rating |
|---|---|

1. Getting the job done
   a) Quality

   b) On time

2. Have fun doing it

3. Talk openly about issues

4. Help one another etc.

Now the group members reflect on why the ratings came out as they did.  They become specific about what they do well and what they do poorly as a team.

*Another Example*

The Third Party asks on what questions would the members like to know the positions of the others.  The group arrives at a set of questions:

○ Should we do something about our relationship with organization X?

○ Am I able to influence what goes on in this organization?

○ Do I plan to leave this organization in the next two years?

Each member jots down a yes or no reply to each question, and then predicts the number of yes and no answers for the total group.  The results are tabulated and posted on the wall:

| | Actual Count | | Predicted Count (range) | |
|---|---|---|---|---|
| Question | Yes | No | Yes | No |
| 1. Organization X | 5 | 5 | 3–8 | 2–7 |
| 2. Influence | 3 | 7 | 1–4 | 6–9 |
| 3. Leaving | 4 | 6 | 2–5 | 5–8 |
| etc. | | | | |

The range of the *predictions* is an indicator of common understanding. The *actual count* starts the group working on some real problems.

*Another Example*

After an effort lasting some period of time, the group has reached a fairly high level of trust and mutual helpfulness. However, one member remarks that he has been troubled by certain relationships among members—and he feels the group has been avoiding the subject.

The Third Party invites each group member to pursue two questions:

○ Which two persons in the group do I *like* working with the *most*?

○ Which two persons in the group do I *like* working with the *least*?

The responses are collected on signed slips of paper and tabulated on a grid as follows:

*Choosers*

| | Bob | Frank | John | Dick | Ken | Mark |
|---|---|---|---|---|---|---|
| Bob | | ✔ | | X | X | X |
| Frank | ✔ | | ✔ | | | ✔ |
| John | ✔ | ✔ | | ✔ | ✔ | ✔ |
| Dick | X | | ✔ | | ✔ | |
| Ken | | X | X | ✔ | | X |
| Mark | X | X | X | X | X | |

*Chosen*

✔ = most    X = least

In the ensuing discussion, the group deals with the intensity of the choices, the reasons for them, and perhaps what sort of conduct can improve the relationships.

*Uses*

Polling is a quick way of bringing buried issues to light. Such issues may be of two types:
○ Those which are interfering with the progress of a meeting.
○ Chronic problems in the organization.

*Benefits*

Polling is fast, interesting, and simple. Anyone can devise his own questions and polling procedure.

The whole group takes part in the process and feels greater commitment to the results. It is an easy way to get issues out into the open, and a good way to move from general, inconclusive discussions to specifics that can be dealt with. It is a highly flexible method that can be improvised to suit the needs of the moment.

*Limitations*

The questions aren't as carefully thought out as those on professionally developed questionnaires, and they don't lend themselves to large groups. They are most useful in groups of 5 to 30.

*Operating Hints*

Don't rush into polling at your next meeting to suit *your* interests. The questions and the procedure must make sense to the group. If not, the responses won't be very useful, and the other members will start wondering about *you*.

Group involvement is important for another reason. As the examples show, polls can touch people where they are quite sensitive. The group's OK to go ahead is the only evidence that they feel up to it.

If sensitive relationships are to be taken up, it's wise to have a competent Third Party present.

Be cautious about secretive methods of collecting information. An occasional secret ballot may be all right, but beware of raising issues which the group is unwilling to confront openly.

Once the questions have been answered, move the discussion to specifics as soon as possible. General discussions leave a lot of fog in the atmosphere.

5.   COLLAGES

Individuals, subgroups, or groups may be asked to prepare collages around a theme (e.g., "How do you feel about this team?", "How do you feel about yourself in this organization, and this organization in the company?", "What is happening to this organization and the team?"). Materials for the collage include large sheets of paper, magazines from which pictures and words may be clipped, crayons, felt pens, glue, scissors, etc. Each finished collage is then described for the total group by the individual or subgroup preparing it. If a single, large collage is prepared by the total group, it becomes the focal point for a total group discussion.

*Uses*

As an instrument for tracing the cultural and emotional topography of a group. The collage allows the members to express themselves to one another on a fairly deep, personal level. Common themes from collages tend to find their way onto group agendas.

*Benefits*

Collages can be quite effective in breaking the ice. Afterwards, the group may be more willing to deal with personal and interpersonal issues. Besides, they are fun to do.

When the group produces a large single collage, the members are apt to be proud of their accomplishment. The experience is unifying.

*Limitations*

Groups that are formal in behavior may resist what first appears to be a children's game.

As noted, collages are highly expressive. On the other hand, they may reveal little that is hard and specific.

*Operating Hints*

Lead boldly into the assignment to help the group overcome its resistance to this "child's play."

If they want, let the participants suggest the theme for the collage. Provide plenty of magazines and ample space, and be prepared to wind up with a cluttered room.

Suggest to the participants that they cut out any pictures or words which "ring a bell" without giving much thought to why they do so.

The time for preparing the collages should be approximately one-half hour to an hour and a half. Judge the time by whether the participants seem productively employed, but apply deadline pressure to discourage excessive deliberation.

Don't let the responses to the presentation turn into a game of interpretation. The object is to understand the presenter without putting words into his mouth and without making him feel defensive.

Have the boss present his collage last so his presentation won't color the others.

6. DRAWINGS

One member of the group (or some, or all members) is asked to make a drawing about an aspect of the individual's life, or something about the nature of the organization. The drawings are made on large sheets of paper posted on the walls. The authors are then asked to discuss their drawings in the presence of the group. Members of the group may ask questions to clarify the author's intent. Common themes and problems, or significant differences of opinion, are then culled from the drawings and posted on chart pads.

Here is an example of an instruction given to all members of a group:

Draw a circle for each person in the group, including your boss and his boss. Make the circle proportionately larger for those individuals who seem to have greater influence over the way the group does its work.

Place the circles near or far apart, depending on how closely you feel those individuals must work together to get their job done. Label the circles with the names of the people.

With a blue line, connect those people who are personally close to one another. Connect with a red line those people who are far apart (i.e., individuals who communicate very little with one another or between whom you feel there is friction).

*Other Examples*

Draw a picture of how it feels to be in your organization.

Draw a picture of your organization today and another picture of what you would like it to be in five years.

The drawings may vary in style from conventional organization charts to imaginative symbolic representations.

*Uses*

Drawings of the sort suggested can be a powerful way of unearthing for the group issues that have been buried alive—for example, the presence of cliques, inappropriate competition, or personal influence contrary to organizational goals. While they may be used to describe a current situation, drawings can also display what people want and hope for in place of what they have now.

Drawings can be used for building an agenda for team-building or similar meetings.

*Benefits*

Pictures are often rich compressions of meaning. Moreover, they are inherently stimulating to work with. Drawings may also afford an easy entry into discussion of tender subjects.

*Limitations*

Drawings are an expressive medium. But they are difficult for some to enter into unless the directions are quite literal and easy to follow.

*Operating Hints*

Don't attempt to cover too many subjects in a single drawing or it will become difficult to understand.

Spend enough time on the instructions so that the members understand the *objectives* of the activity. Don't discourage people from departing from your rules; the individual may do better in his own fashion.

When a person presents his drawing to the group, encourage clarifying questions. *Discourage* general discussion, debate, or clever interpretation of the drawing by other members of the group.

Keep in readiness large sheets of paper, colored markers, and tape.

Some groups need more guidance than others. A group that is esthetically inclined is apt to respond swiftly to the assignment. Others may want more specific instruction.

## 7. PHYSICAL REPRESENTATION OF ORGANIZATIONS

Members of a group are asked to arrange themselves physically in the room according to some group characteristic they are troubled about. For example, if the participants are apparently concerned about cliques, each may be asked to position himself in the room so that he stands nearest to those he feels warmest about and farthest from those he feels coolest about. Or, if inappropriate influence is an issue, they may be asked to arrange themselves closer or further from the boss according to the amount of influence they feel they have. Usually, the manager takes a position in the middle of the room as a starting point. Members are asked to call attention to any aspect of the deployment which they believe to be inaccurate. Usually no further instructions are given. Discussion normally occurs spontaneously.

*Uses*

For bringing into the open relationship issues which are bothering the group. These may include cliques, feelings about being "in" or "out" of the group, influence, competitiveness, communication channels, etc.

*Benefits*

A good, rapid, and dramatic diagnostic tool for disclosing interpersonal issues that are hindering a group.

Creates strong motivation to improve the situation.

*Limitations*

Many groups find this sort of thing too "far out," so the method isn't useful to them, and may do more harm than good.

*Operating Hints*

You will need a qualified Third Party.

# Methods for Better Meetings

This section describes five methods of very broad utility:

○ Chart Pads

○ Going Around the Room

○ Critiquing

○ Subgrouping

○ The Fishbowl

They are arranged in decreasing order of frequency with which they are likely to be used.  You are not apt to overuse them in any event.


## 1.  CHART PADS

Large sheets of paper are a basic tool of group work.  The chart imposes discipline without the need to give orders.  Included are flip charts presented on easels, prepared in advance or on the spot, or sheets mounted on the walls.  Everything significant that occurs in connection with a meeting is posted where it is visible to everyone during the meeting.  Sheets that are useful for follow-up activity are retained.  In most cases, the Third Party does the writing.  In fact, he's usually at loose ends without it.  The boss or any member of the group who feels he can make his point best by using charts should feel free to do so.

*Uses*

Displaying data that were collected before the meeting.

Building and agreeing upon an agenda.

Recording significant ideas or issues that occur during the meeting.

Presenting facts or concepts.

Compiling action lists.

Entertaining or playing with ideas.

*Benefits*

Properly used, charts help people to grasp what's really going on. They also focus the attention of the group, maintain meeting discipline and pace, and impart a sense of direction and movement. They prevent important facts or feelings from slipping away. They fix individual responsibility for action items. They tend to legitimize feeling; i.e., once the feeling is posted, it loses its terror. The process of posting information about feeling tends to moderate intense conflict; it can therefore help group participation. Unlike a blackboard, the chart can be rolled up and taken with you.

*Limitations*

Charts are not always convenient. They may be distracting when the participants are expressing intense feelings.

*Operating Hints*

Don't forget the sticky tape.

Make the chart pads available to everyone in the group.

Invite members to come up to write or change things.

Don't bury important paper on an easel; post it on the walls.

Use the easel freely, but don't post so much material on the wall that it dilutes interest or confuses.

Write boldly and legibly.

The preferred writing instruments are heavy crayons or felt pens.

Use colors effectively. A subjective note: black suggests command and control, red alarm value, and blue optimism.

Use a backing sheet when you're writing with felt pens to avoid marking the walls.

You can later have the charts typed and distributed.

## 2. GOING AROUND THE ROOM

The procedure is simply to go around the room in sequence and ask each person to state his position as of this moment.

*Example*

A manager and his group of 16 are engaged in a one-day meeting to discuss reorganization. They are presently organized as a pool from which the manager makes individual or *ad hoc* group assignments. Now the manager has proposed that they form into four leaderless, self-managing teams. The nature of the work requires that the people in these teams work together very closely under high pressure. There are strong objections in the group to various implications of the proposal. Somehow, the members of each quartet will have to assume responsibility for one another's performance, likes, and dislikes. They will have to perform other functions which traditionally belong to Big Daddy. The discussion has become deadlocked and the Third Party calls a break.

When the group reassembles, the Third Party suggests that they go around the room, with each person stating his position as of this moment. He starts with a junior member of the group who has said very little until now.

The junior member remarks: "I guess I don't understand the amount of feeling. As I interpret the proposal, the kind of relationships we are talking about are only the kind we need to do the best job anyway." His matter-of-fact interpretation suddenly reduces apprehension. As each person speaks, it becomes evident that the group is prepared to give the proposal a trial.

*Uses*

When the group is hung up around the views of those who are dominating the conversation.

When the group seems to have run out of solutions.

To take a reading of where the group is at key points in a meeting.

An excellent way to wind up a meeting.

*Benefits*

Prevents domination by a few.

Helps bring the less outspoken people into the action and into the team.   You never know when someone is sitting there with the answer.

Generally turns the conversation into more productive channels.

As a wrap-up to a meeting, this procedure can be very powerful; it shakes loose important issues that people have not gotten up their nerve to bring up before, frequently brings out some innovative ideas that have been gestating, and produces a wave of positive feedback and personal commitment that helps cement the group. "Going Around the Room" at the end of a good meeting can be a moving experience.

*Limitations*

If the level of trust in the group is low, the method may turn people off.

*Operating Hints*

Use it often except as noted under "Limitations."   It's almost impossible to get an overdose.

Start with those who haven't been heard from.

3.   CRITIQUING

A critique is a comment on what's going on.   It may occur spontaneously:

"Hold it! We're going too fast."

or

"Hey, when are we gonna do what we came here for?"

Or you can plan for the critique by setting aside a little time for the participants to reflect aloud on what they've been doing.

*Example*

Bored and irritated by his own staff meetings, the manager determines to change them. At the end of the next three staff meetings, he goes around the room asking each person to comment on:

○ The liveliness of the meeting.

○ Its usefulness and pertinence.

○ Proposed changes in meeting style, content, or format.

Later, the staff plans a few changes. They agree to:

○ Call different sorts of meetings for different purposes (e.g., information, problem solving, etc.).

○ Invite only those members of the staff to whom that meeting's subject means a lot.

○ Modify their regular meeting schedule.

○ Call meetings only when needed.

○ Meet less often (hurray!).

*Another Example*

Time for critiques is scheduled at intervals during a lengthy management training session. The "students" speak up as to which subject matter they need more of, and which less.

*Uses*

Routinely, as a measurement of the effectiveness of an activity. Critiquing is also a way of infusing life into tedious proceedings, and a counter for people who keep asking for more meetings, whereas you know there are already too many.  Finally, critiques act as check-points during a long session.

*Benefits*

Critiquing is simple and fast.  It distributes responsibility for effectiveness among all participants instead of loading it on the manager's back.  Many of the listeners will at last speak their piece.  Finally, critiquing usually improves manners.

*Limitations*

Like anything else, the critique can become an empty ritual.  If the real culprit of the meeting is the boss, and no one volunteers to "bell the cat," well!  The agony only intensifies.

*Operating Hints*

Keep critique time short—one to two minutes per person.

Reserve time for critiques.

Avoid "working problems" during the critique, or using it to sneak in the last word.

Encourage cheers for what was good about the activity as well as boos for what went wrong.

Encourage everyone to take part.

Should the critique become a regular feature of your meetings, urge people to comment right *now* about how the group is doing, not wait until it's all over.

If the group agrees to certain changes but somehow no changes ever take place, the critiques will take on a tone of futility.  The purpose of the critique is to get feedback as a step toward making something better, not to let people blow off steam.

4.  SUBGROUPING

The group is temporarily divided into subgroups of two to six people.  The subgroups are assigned individual topics or a common discussion topic.  Each subgroup then summarizes its discussion to the reassembled total group.  The information is then discussed by the total group.

*Example*

In a team-building meeting, the participants included professional and clerical employees.  To surface underlying issues for the agenda, the group was divided into homogeneous subgroups.  Each sub-group reported its proposed agenda items.  For the first time, the voices of the clerical staff were clearly heard.

*Uses*

A way of collecting information on current conditions within the organization, or desired changes.

Building an agenda, working on agenda items, setting priorities.

A way of making progress when the total group is stuck.

*Benefits*

Subgrouping is faster than working in a large group.

It keeps people involved in what is going on.  (They can get lost in the large group.)

It gives every member a chance to be heard—more air time—and permits a wide sampling of information, ideas, and opinions.

*Limitations*

Some of the information imparted in the subgroups will be lost or blurred by secondhand transmittal when it is reported to the total group.  If it is important for the group as a whole to participate in an event or experience, don't subgroup.

Subgrouping can introduce intergroup phenomena (e.g., competi-tion) which may or may not be relevant to your purposes.  The more intense and long-lived the subgroup experience, the more likely will the subgroup insist on its independence of the total group.  It may then be necessary to provide special means for "bridging" to the other subgroups.

### Operating Hints

*Resistance:* Groups generally resist dividing into subgroups. It's worth pushing, however, because the experience is usually satisfying.

*Size:* The smaller the group, the greater the *intensity*. There tends to be more *action* as the group approaches five or six members.

*Homogeneous* groups make it easier for individuals to talk. *Heterogeneous* groups have the advantage of collecting more divergent views, hence of facilitating constructive conflict. By including people from different groups to deal with common problems, you can help them to work together collaboratively about these problems.

*Selection:* If you feel it's important to form subgroups of people who like to work together, have them select their own groups. Otherwise, appoint members according to some principle (e.g., representativeness, grouping the quiet people or mixing them with live wires, homogeneity or heterogeneity, organizational unit, etc.).

The leader should be prepared to explain the basis for selection if the group is uncomfortable with his choices and challenges him as to his reasons.

Make sure each subgroup understands its assignment and selects a reporter. The output of each subgroup should be presented on chart pads.

Consolidate information for an agenda or an action list, etc. This can be done by the leader of the total group (top manager present or Third Party), by the subgroup reporters, or by a special group assigned for this purpose.

*Bridging:* Reconvening and reporting what happened is the most common way of tying together the experience of the subgroups. Another way is to post on the wall the products of each subgroup so that everyone can see them and discuss them informally. Another way is to form new cross-representational subgroups for the next stage of business. Another way is pairing members of different groups.

The subgroup may work more effectively if it appoints one of its members or an outsider as a Third Party. This is particularly true if the life of the subgroup exceeds an hour.

5. THE FISHBOWL

The attendees arrange themselves in concentric circles:

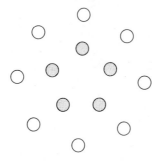

The persons in the inner circle (the Fishbowl) take the active role; the outer circle consists of observers whose task is to listen and who are relatively inactive.

*Uses*

To disseminate information from the Fishbowl group to a larger group which is not directly involved.

*Example:* A new top team for a major project forms a Fishbowl to make itself and its views known to lower levels of management.

To develop information within one group and transmit it to a second group, where the second group is directly involved but needs simply to listen for an interval.

*Example:* The Organization Mirror (pages 101–105) in which representatives of several organizations form a Fishbowl to provide feedback on the performance of another organizational unit, at its request, while members of the latter organization take up the observer/listener role in the outer circle.

To work on solving a problem in the Fishbowl group when the assistance of the observers is desired.

*Example:* A meeting between two organizations intended to improve their working relationships. A subgroup, made up of agents of both groups, is charged with settling an important and difficult issue between the groups. The subgroup meets in the Fishbowl and is surrounded by the two larger groups. Every 20 minutes or so, the action in the Fishbowl is stopped. The observers now (1) evaluate the effectiveness of the subgroup members in helping one another and (2) make suggestions for solving the problem.

*Benefits*

As a method of transmitting information, the spontaneous quality of the Fishbowl lends interest.

Those in the outer circle are given an especially good opportunity to observe and to understand the members in the Fishbowl.

The technique affords the advantage of a small group efficiency simultaneously with delivery of information to a larger group.

The presence of the observers places a healthy pressure on the inner circle to stick to the point. The subject matter is controlled and the discussion tends to be orderly.

When the Fishbowl is critiqued, all participants can learn effective ways of working in small groups.

*Limitations*

Not good when a carefully planned presentation is needed. Some people have trouble working in a Fishbowl in front of others and may resent the process. It can be frustrating to the observers unless provision is made for their participation.

*Operating Hints*

Be sure the observers can hear and see what's going on in the Fishbowl.  Sometimes a semicircle may be better than a circle.

Be sure everyone understands the objectives, the procedure, and his role in it.

Whenever possible, provide for observer participation, that is, for critiquing and making suggestions.  One move is to place an empty chair in the Fishbowl.  An observer who has something to say, or a question to ask, may take this chair briefly and become a temporary member of the Fishbowl.

If the Fishbowl is developing points for future action, someone should make notes on chart pads posted where the whole group can see.

# Methods for Changing
# the Quality of Relationships

The seven methods presented in this section are used for surfacing hidden issues between people and moving toward a more healthy relationship. They include:

○ Role Playing

○ Getting Acquainted

○ Hearing

○ Positive Feedback

○ Making Deals (Out on the Table)

○ Likes and Reservations

○ Nonverbal Encounters

These are not arranged in any order. They are approximately equal in utility, and they are more or less confronting depending on how they are used.

1.  ROLE PLAYING

In role playing, we act out a short scene. The scene may be in the past or present, or one that is still to come. Members of the group substitute for one or more of the principals. In a replay, the principals may play themselves.

When the scene has been acted out, or if the players reach an impasse, the group engages in a critique of the enactment. If the problem has not yet been worked through, others may then assume the roles in a replay of the drama.

In a variation termed *role reversals,* a subordinate may take the part of his boss, and vice versa. Or two managers of equal status who are in conflict may first play themselves, then each other.

Another variation is *alter ego,* in which one member attempts to give voice to the hidden feelings of another.

○ *Uses*

Role playing is effective when there is confusion about what is going on in a relationship and the parties desire to learn; when rationality and understanding have been replaced by heat or withdrawal; or when someone is having difficulty in understanding others or expressing himself. Typical occasions include the following:

○ After a discussion, the boss feels frustrated and the employee feels disappointed and misunderstood.
○ Two key people have battled inconclusively over who has responsibility for what.
○ A manager has scheduled a two-hour meeting with the big boss to gain his support for an important change. He is pessimistic about his ability to handle himself well in the meeting.

*Benefits*

Role playing tends to move the group to a positive outcome. The technique fosters empathy and group support; it tends to guide the principal to a more objective view of himself.

Role playing is highly stimulating because it lifts interpersonal feelings to the surface.

As members begin to identify with the principals in their conflicts, the group tends to pull together and act helpfully.

*Limitations*

*Time:* It may take half an hour to an hour of role playing before the members get into it deeply enough for the experience to be worthwhile.

Some individuals simply won't put themselves into the role of another. In this situation, the enactment is apt to be superficial.

*Operating Hints*

An impasse between two or more individuals is a cue to consider role playing.

In casting actors, look to the members who have been empathetic to the principals. Or ask.

Suggest that the actors change their position in the room. An actor might take the chair of the person whose role he assumes. An alter ego might stand behind the principal, or sit in front of him.

Start the drama with the event (past, present, or future) which seems most critical to the problem.

As director, press on persistently.

Everyone in the room may explode into advice-giving. Discourage it.

If the players reach a deadlock, reverse roles or switch actors. Substitute actors if someone looks promising. Get in yourself, if necessary.

Once the principals and the group begin to grasp what has been happening in the relationship, consider a replay in which the actors put to use what has been learned.

After the drama, encourage the group to discuss and summarize the lessons learned.

A skilled Third Party can help a group get the most from role playing. But you can't go far wrong even without him.

## 2.  GETTING ACQUAINTED

Everyone pairs off with a person he does not know very well and asks a personal question or two of the other. A time limit is set.

Sample questions:

○ What do you like or dislike about your job?

○ What are your career or life objectives?

○ What do you like or dislike about the way you do your job?

○ Who are you?

○ What's your life been like?

After the group is brought back together, each member introduces and describes his partner to all.

This sort of interviewing may also be done in clusters of three or more if the questions are less personal and of narrower scope. The introductions can be made to a subgroup if the overall group is massive. The composition of the subgroups can be reshuffled and the process repeated until each member has been introduced to everyone else.

## Uses

To help strangers acquire a revealing quick impression of everyone else. But the technique also awakens fresh interest among people who have worked together for a long time.

The method is useful for building an agenda. (Question: "What do you hope to get out of this meeting?") The Getting Acquainted method can be useful when a meeting is going poorly because of distrust, competition, etc. (for example, a meeting between two groups with a history of unfriendly relations). The method helps in setting up a new team quickly.

## Benefits

A fast and effective way of converting strangers to friends, of overcoming isolation or dispelling hostility. It livens the conversation. It gives all participants a chance to influence the course of the next hours.

*Limitations*

In a large meeting, everyone cannot be introduced to everyone else in this way without time-consuming repetition.

Improperly used, the method can introduce an air of false amity. ("Now, folks, the rule is to get acquainted and be friends, so we'll be friends even if it hurts.")

*Operating Hints*

Explain the entire procedure in advance so that everyone knows what's coming and how much time he has.

Choose the sort of interview question that suits the purpose of the gathering and its level of trust. Certain topics may take longer than makes sense; others may be too superficial or too personal. Listen to the group. If the group members don't like the interview questions you propose, there may be a good reason.

If the information is to be used to help form the agenda, record significant information from the introductions on chart pads.

To speed the process, use the largest feasible groupings for interviewing and for introductions.

3.  HEARING

> *"He never spares himself in conversation. He gives himself so generously that hardly anybody else is permitted to give anything in his presence."*
>
> *Aneurin Bevan of Churchill*

*Example*

George and Tom are battling endlessly and without stint. It is apparent to the onlookers that they are better at talking than at listening. Mounting hostility makes them deafer still. What, if anything, can you hope to do?

*Step 1.*  First you must claim their attention. As Ring Lardner put it: "'Shut up!' he explained."

*Step 2.* Dare them to say that they are truly hearing each other, and swiftly ask them to prove it. A rigorous test: bid each to repeat the other's statement until he can do it to the latter's satisfaction.

*Step 3.* Ask George and Tom to talk about their feelings for a while instead of the argument.

*Step 4.* If they can't, consider asking the group members to help by offering their view of the disagreement, or by Role Playing (especially the *alter ego* type, page 169).

### Another Example

The meeting is following its usual course. Tom, Dick, and Harry are, as usual, dominating the conversation. Fred says something in a low voice and no one listens. Casper finally ventures and is cut off.

The Third Party calls attention to these incidents and there is a debate as to who is responsible, the speaker (or nonspeaker) or the listener. Solution: It's a joint responsibility.

The method is simple: call attention to specific cases where people are not hearing each other.

### Uses

The method may be used, as appropriate, in any kind of meeting, including one specially arranged for this purpose. Thus George and Tom may meet with a Third Party for ear therapy.

### Benefits

Breaks up wandering or downright injurious discussions. Converts controversy to collaboration.

Improves hearing skills and the group's ability to face up to social deafness.

Helps bring the quiet ones into the group.

> *"You don't have a team until everyone's been heard."*
>
> *Attributed to Arturo Toscanini*

*Limitations*

It takes time.

It's sometimes hard to get people to do it.

*Operating Hints*

Don't march through the series of steps beyond a point of real need. If Step 1 or 2 does the job, stop there. If antagonism and distrust are rampant, start working with the feelings involved.

Be forceful and persistent. You'll probably have to be.

### 4.  POSITIVE FEEDBACK

In the sense used here, feedback is letting the other fellow know how you are receiving his signals. Positive feedback means telling him you approve of something about him or something he's done. It sounds simple, but it is extremely stimulating and intense.

*Example*

Johnson was distraught. It was near the end of the *third* business meeting with those other groups, and *still* everyone was deadlocked. He told them off—and good!

Someone suggested they go around the table for half an hour. Ground rule: each man says something positive about the others.

Five minutes of shocked silence followed. Wilson said it was a crazy idea, but he was shushed by the others. After a slow start, they did it—and adjourned. In their next meeting they got their business done quickly.

*Uses*

In a deadlock. There is an atmosphere of recrimination. The group has already tried critiquing but the results have been negative. The situation is tense and your prediction of the outcome is gloomy.

When someone asks for feedback and you think it's going to be rough for him to take, start first with positive feedback, or mix in the positive with the negative.

When you want to find out if what you're doing is being taken as you intended.

When a group is dispirited.

As a normal part of everyday communication or as a change of pace.

*Benefits*

People feel warmer, less guarded, more powerful, and readier to do things cooperatively.

*Limitations*

Many people have trouble accepting praise and are made extremely uncomfortable by flattery.  A hint of insincerity leads to despair.  Also, positive feedback may be confused with manipulative compliments.

*Operating Hints*

Set clear ground rules on length of time; make sure that participation is voluntary.

It's surprisingly hard to do and needs careful policing.  After the easy openers, it gets tough and the more comfortable "buts" creep in.  Don't permit negative feedback. The main benefits come from keeping at it when the sledding is rough.  Encourage the groups to keep going for the agreed-upon time.

Debrief when the exercise is over to work out any unresolved feelings (including negative ones) and questions.

Positive feedback can also be self-feedback.  We often weaken ourselves by worrying about our deficiencies.  As this happens, people and groups lose their sense of power. If a group seems to be suffering from this failure, try self-feedback. Ask each person to answer a question like, "When do I feel most effective?" or "What part of my job do I get the most fun out of?" or "When do I feel most influential?"

## 5.  MAKING DEALS (OUT ON THE TABLE)

Two persons, in the presence of others, negotiate what they want from each other and what they feel they can and want to give to each other. In general, they are asked to negotiate around questions such as:

○ What do you want from each other in connection with your work?

○ How do you feel you can and want to help each other with your work?

○ What do you want from each other personally (e.g., moral support, not saying things behind one's back, friendship, respect)?

The group assists the negotiation by helping the pair to be as clear as possible about what they want (not easy), and by furnishing insight, ideas, and encouragement to help the pair reach a mutually beneficial "deal."

### Example

At a team-building meeting, John and Paul are having an inconclusive and somewhat acrimonious discussion about the company's poor relations with a customer whom Paul deals with. The group grows increasingly restive. The Third Party breaks in and outlines the procedure and questions for making a deal. John and Paul agree to try it, and 10 minutes later the underlying issues begin to come out so they can be confronted. Paul agrees that John has some ideas that could be helpful but he objects to having them rammed down his throat; John feels unfairly slighted and wants very much to be respected by Paul as a person with ideas and initiative.

*Another Example*

At the start of a team-building meeting, the Third Party reports that the premeeting interviews show that each person in the group sees himself as operating independently but many are not satisfied with the kind of support they are giving the others. He suggests going around the room, with each man in turn negotiating with the others around the three questions, which he writes on a chart pad. He posts another sheet of paper on the wall for each man, with his name at the top of it. These sheets are used to record any commitments to action that come out of the negotiations. Each man keeps his sheet for his own follow-up.

*Uses*

As part of the framework of a team-building meeting.

To clarify and work through ambiguous exchanges and troublesome relationships in a group.

*Benefits*

Much of the interpersonal garbage in a group arises from our not being outspoken and explicit about what we want. Also, we are not clear in our own minds as to what we want, or we use indirect and manipulative methods for getting our way. We all have our game: verbally crushing the opposition, office politics, "I am a nice guy so be nice to me," and so on. All of these tactics breed misunderstanding and mistrust. Making Deals is a step toward replacing cute games with direct, man-to-man negotiation.

It is a systematic way for focusing attention on the many positive ways in which we can help one another. Because the people involved decide what issues are raised or not raised, the method suits itself to their readiness to deal with tough issues.

*Limitations*

The corollary to the last point above is that this is a relatively superficial method. A skilled Third Party can make it penetrating. It takes a long time to get around a group using this method.

*Operating Hints*

Keep it moving.  Here are some ways:

○ Cut off the negotiation and move on if it's really superficial.  The participants, in front of the group, may feel pressured to make commitments or explore possibilities that don't really engage them.

Particularly if the group is large:

○ Don't have each person negotiate with everyone.  Have him select several who are most important to him.  Work in subgroups.  Limit the negotiations to one item for each question.

○ Vary the question to suit the need.  For example, in setting up a team for a new task, the key question might be, "What are my biggest concerns about how the two of us will work together?"

○ Be sure the negotiators are hearing each other.  If there is any doubt, have one repeat what he thinks the other is asking of him.  (Refer to Hearing, pages 172–174).

○ If you're Going Around the Room (pages 157–158), save the boss and his negotiations until last, when people are warmed up.  This also serves as a wrap-up.

6.   LIKES AND RESERVATIONS

> *"I look at you and I see rebellion.  I see the scars of liquor and dope.  I see pain and reckless abandon.  Oh, Ronald, it's such a good face."*
>
> W. F. Brown

In a team-building meeting, each participant in turn picks another person in the group and makes two statements to him: "Something I like about you is . . ." and "A reservation I have about you is. . ." After each statement, the recipient repeats it until the sender feels he has been heard correctly.  There is no discussion until each participant has had his turn as a sender.

*Uses*

To break the ice. Specifically prescribed for "nice" groups who have trouble talking about the inevitable hitches in their human relations.

As a quick and dirty way for the group to diagnose its relationships.

When the tone of a meeting is shallow and people are not vitally involved. As a stimulus, and perhaps a lead-in to what's going on below the surface.

*Benefits*

Gets everyone in the swim.

The act of repeating stresses accurate hearing and offsets defensiveness.

By requiring rounded communication (both positive and negative), the method raises trust in the group.

As a means of bringing relationship problems to the surface, it has several advantages over premeeting interviewing:

- It is faster.
- It is out in the open, not anonymous.
- It brings to light those issues the group is ready to deal with, and not those which are too hot for it to handle. It is more reliable than the judgment of most individual interviewers.
- The information brought to light is clearly the group members' own and not something an interviewer is telling to them.

*Limitations*

By using interview data, a skilled Third Party may be able to help the group deal with tougher and more important issues than will be brought to light by this method.

Likes and Reservations is not equally suited to all types of groups. For example, a group which is highly competitive, combative, and free with its criticism should begin with a method that emphasizes warmth, such as Getting Acquainted (pages 170–172).

*Operating Hints*

Insist that the group follow the repeat procedure, even though it may seem unnecessary and awkward at first. After the round of sending and receiving is completed, start the general discussion by critiquing (pages 160–162) what happened. For example, who received the most messages, who got none? (You may want to open up the sending and receiving again briefly so those left out may be brought in.) Or what seemed most important to the receivers, the likes or the reservations? Or what seemed most important to the senders? (Critiquing helps avoid underemphasis.)

## 7. NONVERBAL ENCOUNTERS

> *"First let them do their verbals. Then they can have their nonverbals."*
>
> *Teenybopper Group Leader*

The team-building meeting makes no progress because two of the key people, Bob and Bill, can't agree on their respective roles and relationships. Each defends his own "territory" and his own people. The argument is apparently rational, but in a subtle way each seems to be trying to put the other down. Noting the unyielding stare exchanged between them, the Third Party proposes that they Indian wrestle. Once they start, they put everything into it. Bob catches Bill off balance and spills him to the floor. Discomfited, Bill says, "Two out of three." He wins the next fall, and Bob the third. "I'll buy you a drink," says Bob. It seems to make little difference who wins. Both are winded and relaxed. The ensuing discussion is more free, exploratory, and positive.

This is only one of hundreds of nonverbal methods. (Refer to the Bibliography.) There are many nonverbal exercises of varying degrees of intimacy for dealing with:

○ Getting acquainted.

○ Feeling left out of a group.

○ Feelings about dependence and authority.

○ Bringing the members of a group closer together on a personal level.

○ Inhibitions.

○ Trust.

○ Competitiveness.

○ Cooperation.

○ Feelings about status and power.

○ Aggressiveness.

*Uses*

When words fail.

To loosen up communications.

To interject some life and fun.

*Benefits*

We use words to communicate. We are also very skillful at using them not to communicate, to hide from ourselves or others. We clarify with logic. We also befuddle ourselves with logic.

Actions speak louder than words—also more clearly and more truthfully.

Nonverbal methods help to:

○ Disclose underlying feelings that are driving us.

○ Foster the expression of these feelings in constructive ways.

○ Relieve tensions that block communications and suppress energy.

○ Bring people closer together.

Properly used, nonverbal techniques can be quite useful and powerful. They are not superficial, although their simple format may make them appear so.

*Limitations*

They may not go over in a conservative group or organization. To many people these methods appear awkward, inappropriate, embarrassing, childish, or even frightening. These feelings limit the usefulness of nonverbal methods.

In certain quarters, nonverbal exercises have become so "in" that they have been carried to ridiculous extremes and have begun to assume a shallow and mechanical quality.

*Operating Hints*

Don't do it just because you think it's jazzy. Be clear about how it will help the group accomplish *its* objective.

Conduct yourself in a positive and confident manner when you introduce a nonverbal method.

Timing and appropriateness are critical. Nonverbal techniques are effective at the right moment, mechanical at the wrong time.

In team-building, a conservative rule to follow is to watch for signs that the group is unable to deal with a strong feeling verbally, *then* consider what nonverbal method may help.

# Bibliography

# Bibliography

## I. About Man: Some Points of View that Underlie O.D.

McGregor, Douglas, *The Human Side of Enterprise,* McGraw-Hill, New York, 1960.

Maslow, A. H., *Motivation and Personality,* Harper and Brothers, New York, 1954.

Rogers, Carl R., *On Becoming a Person,* Houghton Mifflin, Boston, 1961.

## II. O.D.: What's It All About?

Bennis, Warren G., *Organization Development: Its Nature, Origins, and Prospects,* Addison-Wesley, Reading, Mass., 1969.

## III. Approaches to O.D.: Strategy and Tactics

Beckhard, Richard, *Organization Development: Strategies and Models,* Addison-Wesley, Reading, Mass., 1969.

Blake, Robert R., and Jane Srygley Mouton, *Building a Dynamic Corporation Through Grid Organization Development,* Addison-Wesley, Reading, Mass., 1969.

Lawrence, Paul R., and Jay W. Lorsch, *Developing Organizations: Diagnosis and Action,* Addison-Wesley, Reading, Mass., 1969.

## IV. Consultant/Third Party: Role and Skills

Schein, Edgar H., *Process Consultation: Its Role in Organization Development*, Addison-Wesley, Reading, Mass., 1969.

Walton, Richard E., *Interpersonal Peacemaking: Confrontations and Third-Party Consultation*, Addison-Wesley, Reading, Mass., 1969.

## V. Related Training Tools: Nonverbal Techniques, Management Games, Human Relations Training Exercises, Lectures

Nylen, Donald, Robert J. Mitchell, and Anthony Stout, *Handbook of Staff Development and Human Relations Training: Materials Developed for Use in Africa*, NTL Institute for Applied Behavioral Science, Washington, D.C., 1967.

Pfeiffer, J. William, and John E. Jones, *A Handbook of Structured Experiences for Human Relations Training*, Vols. I and II, University Associates Press, Iowa City, Ia., 1969, 1970.

## VI. What's Going On in the Field of O.D.?

NTL Institute for Applied Behavioral Science, 1201 16th Street N.W., Washington, D.C. 20036.

The Institute provides training programs and some consulting services in O.D., offers publications (including a newsletter and the *Journal of Applied Behavioral Science*), and supports the Organization Development Network, which provides a meeting place for representatives of organizations with O.D. programs.

## VII. Other References in the Text

Atkins, Stuart, and Arthur Kuriloff, "T-Group for a Work Team," *Journal of Applied Behavioral Science*, Vol. 2, No. 1, 1966.

Auspitz, Josiah Lee, "For A Moderate Majority," *Playboy*, April 1970.

Davis, Sheldon A., "An Organic Problem-Solving Method of Organizational Change," *Journal of Applied Behavioral Science*, Vol. 3, No. 1, 1967.

Fleming, Louis B., "Pope Hears Cardinal Challenge Emphasis on Papal Primacy," *Los Angeles Times*, October 14, 1969.

Gardner, John W., article in "Sunday Opinion" section, *Los Angeles Times,* December 1, 1968.

Margulies, Newton, and Anthony P. Raia, "Action Research and the Consultative Process," *Business Perspectives,* Fall 1968, pp. 26–30.

# Index

# Index